KT-173-593

Sandy Berger's Great Age Guide to Online Travel
Copyright © 2007 by Que

International Standard Book Number-10: 0-7897-3571-7

Internation Standard Book Number-13: 978-0-7897-3571-3

Printed in the United States of America

First Printing: February 2007

09   08   07   4   3   2   1

Trademarks

All terms mentioned in this book that are known to be trademarks or service marks have been appropriately capitalized. Que Publishing cannot attest to the accuracy of this information. Use of a term in this book should not be regarded as affecting the validity of any trademark or service mark.

Warning and Disclaimer

Every effort has been made to make this book as complete and as accurate as possible, but no warranty or fitness is implied. The information provided is on an "as is" basis. The author and the publisher shall have neither liability nor responsibility to any person or entity with respect to any loss or damages arising from the information contained in this book.

Bulk Sales

Que Publishing offers excellent discounts on this book when ordered in quantity for bulk purchases or special sales. For more information, please contact

U.S. Corporate and Government Sales
1-800-382-3419
corpsales@pearsontechgroup.com

For sales outside of the U.S., please contact

International Sales
international@pearsoned.com

                    Library of Congress Cataloging-in-Publication Data

Berger, Sandy.

   Great age guide to online travel / Sandy Berger. -- 1st ed.

     p. cm.

   ISBN 0-7897-3571-7

1. Travel--Computer network resources. 2. Internet. 3. World Wide Web. I. Title.

G155.A1B437 2007

025.06'91--dc22

                         2007000910

ASSOCIATE PUBLISHER
Greg Wiegand

ACQUISITIONS EDITOR
Stephanie J. McComb

DEVELOPMENT EDITOR
Laura Norman

MANAGING EDITOR
Patrick Kanouse

PROJECT EDITOR
Mandie Frank

COPY EDITOR
Gayle Johnson

INDEXER
Ken Johnson

PROOFREADER
Linda Seifert

TECHNICAL EDITOR
Teresa Reynolds

PUBLISHING COORDINATOR
Cindy Teeters

DESIGNER
Anne Jones

PAGE LAYOUT
Bronkella Publishing

Sandy Berger's
Great Age Guide to Online Travel

Contents at a Glance

800 East 96th Street,
Indianapolis, Indiana 46240 USA

Safari **This Book Is Safari Enabled**

Table of Contents

About the Author

Sandy Berger, nationally respected computer authority, journalist, media guest, speaker, and author, has more than three decades of experience as a computer and technology expert.

As president of a nationally recognized computer consulting and training company, Sandy applies her unique ability to explain in easy-to-understand language how to use and enjoy today's technology. Her trademark, "Compu-KISS®," which stands for "The Computer World: Keeping It Short and Simple," represents her approach to helping others enhance their lives through the use of computers and technology. Her popular Compu-KISS website is at www.compukiss.com.

With seven years experience as the primary content provider and host of AARP's Computers and Technology website, Sandy keeps her finger on the pulse of the boomer and zoomer community. Her feature stories, product reviews, and computer tips have brought special insight and ease of use to millions of people who didn't grow up with computers.

Sandy has been a guest on hundreds of radio and television shows, including NBC's *Today Show*, NBC News, CBS News, Fox News, ABC News, WGN, and WOR radio.

Sandy is an excellent example of her own philosophy—use technology, but keep it short and simple. Her previous books adhere to these principles. They include *How to Have a Meaningful Relationship with Your Computer, Your Official Grown-up's Guide to AOL and the Internet, Cyber Savers: Tips & Tricks for Today's Drowning Computer Users, Sandy Berger's Great Age Guide to Better Living Through Technology, Sandy Berger's Great Age Guide to the Internet, Sandy Berger's Great Age Guide to Gadgets & Gizmos,* and *Sandy Berger's Great Age Guide to Online Health & Wellness.*

Sandy is a consumer advocate promoting simplicity, ease of use, and stability in consumer technology products. She works with hardware and software developers to help them make their products more user-friendly.

A cum laude graduate of Chicago's DePaul University, Sandy went on to complete intensive IBM training in computer systems, analysis, programming, system operations, and numerous computer languages. She subsequently applied her expertise within several major corporations before founding Computer Living Corp.

Dedication

This book is dedicated to all those who actively seek out new mind-expanding adventures on the Internet, as well as in the air and on roads, paths, rails, and waterways.

Acknowledgments

Travel adventures often add excitement to what might otherwise be dull, drab lives. This book was created to help you make the most of those adventures by providing resources that can make any trip an exciting and successful journey.

The writing of this book was also an adventure. I want to thank the team at Que. They made this *Great Age Guide* series and, in particular, this *Online Travel* book possible, and they helped turn it into a successful expedition.

Special thanks to Paul Boger, Greg Wiegand, Stephanie McComb, Laura Norman, Teresa Reynolds, Mandie Frank, Gayle Johnson, and Cindy Teeters.

Special thanks to my daughter, Marybeth, for her guidance, and to my wonderful husband, Dave, and to my family for their support and encouragement during the writing of this book.

We Want to Hear from You!

As the reader of this book, *you* are our most important critic and commentator. We value your opinion and want to know what we're doing right, what we could do better, what areas you'd like to see us publish in, and any other words of wisdom you're willing to pass our way.

As an associate publisher for Que Publishing, I welcome your comments. You can email or write me directly to let me know what you did or didn't like about this book—as well as what we can do to make our books better.

Please note that I cannot help you with technical problems related to the topic of this book. We do have a User Services group, however, where I will forward specific technical questions related to the book.

When you write, please be sure to include this book's title and author as well as your name, email address, and phone number. I will carefully review your comments and share them with the author and editors who worked on the book.

Email: feedback@quepublishing.com

Mail: Greg Wiegand
Associate Publisher
Que Publishing
800 East 96th Street
Indianapolis, IN 46240 USA

Reader Services

Visit our website and register this book at www.quepublishing.com/register for convenient access to any updates, downloads, or errata that might be available for this book.

Have you ever stopped to think about the role of technology in your life? There's no doubt that today's younger generations will benefit from current and future technological advances, but today's older generations are already seeing the biggest lifestyle improvements ever. We are living longer, more active lives than our parents and grandparents. Our ancestors went from youth to middle age to old age. We, with a new mentality and the help of technology, have added an entire epoch to our lives—the Great Age!

Everyone knows that the term *baby boomer* refers to individuals born after World War II. This group is generally recognized as encompassing everyone who was born between 1946 and 1964. The boomers' older siblings don't have a moniker associated with their generation, but along with the boomers, they are often called "zoomers" because they are not ready to be relegated to a rocking chair. Boomers and zoomers are zooming into the latter part of their lives, zooming into technology, and zooming into everything they do. They are vibrant individuals who deal enthusiastically with all aspects of their lives. They are ready to sit back and enjoy the Great Age they have created.

About Sandy Berger's Great Age Series

It's about time someone addressed the issues that face those of us who did not grow up with computers. We are not technologically impaired. We are not dummies. And we are not about to be overlooked.

It's just that we didn't learn about computers in school, so we sometimes approach the newfangled digital world with a bit of trepidation. Can someone please tell us just what we need to know without any mumbo jumbo?

That is exactly what this series does. It is geared toward the needs and wants of baby boomers and beyond. It tells you just what you need to know—no more and no less. It uses the winning formula of need-to-know information, along with easy-to-understand explanations.

Over the past decade I have helped many boomers and their older siblings learn how to use computers and technology to enhance and improve their lives. I understand the needs and wants of this generation. After all, I am enjoying the Great Age myself. So I am eager to help guide you into the world of technology, where the "Great Age" is full of enjoyment and anticipation.

Guide to Online Travel

Many of us have watched our parents and grandparents retire and grow old. They grew old gracefully. We want to grow old magnificently. We want our latter years to be happier, more exciting, and livelier than those of our ancestors.

To that end, we are not willing to pass our time sitting in a rocking chair— unless we find a rocking chair overlooking a golf course in North Carolina, a mountain pass in Switzerland, or a stream in Mississippi during one of our many adventures. We are hopping onto planes, trains, ships, motorcycles, automobiles, and even kayaks to explore America and the rest of the world.

The Internet and other high-tech tools can help us plan our trip, get the best prices, and even keep us from getting lost during our journey. This book is filled with information to help us make our adventures easier, more exciting, and more fun.

What's Inside

There are no special instructions for using this book. Start at the beginning, or jump around as you please. It doesn't matter if you're using a PC or a Mac. Much of this book pertains to both. If there are differences, they are noted.

Each chapter begins with a quote, because we can always learn from others. I've also included several special features to help you in your quest for knowledge:

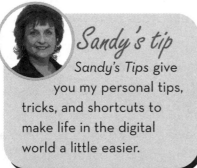

Sandy's tip
Sandy's Tips give you my personal tips, tricks, and shortcuts to make life in the digital world a little easier.

LINGO
Lingo boxes explain high-tech terms in easy-to-understand language.

BLOOPER ALERT
Blooper Alerts help you avoid pitfalls. By telling you about some of the places where most people stumble, these alerts allow you to stay out of trouble and feel a whole lot smarter.

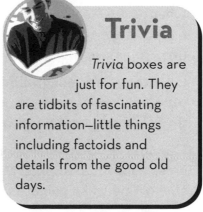

Trivia
Trivia boxes are just for fun. They are tidbits of fascinating information—little things including factoids and details from the good old days.

How This Book Is Organized

- Chapter 1, "The Internet: An Amazing Travel Tool," will help you to understand and utilize available Internet tools to make your travel and travel planning easier and more fun.

- Chapter 2, "Planning Your Trip," is easier than ever before. Internet resources will give you ideas and help you plan your trip.

- Chapter 3, "Bargains Galore," Comparison-shopping for travel bargains can save you money if you know where to look.

- Chapter 4, "Tips for Air and Sea Travel," You can not only get the best price on tickets but you can also get tips on air and sea travel in this chapter.

- Chapter 5, "On the Road Again," More than 80% of Americans vacation by car, motorcycle, or RV. This chapter will help you get the most out of high-tech tools and Internet resources to make that vacation a winner.

- Chapter 6, "Distinctive Travel Adventures," Hiking, kayaking, rock climbing, space travel...if your pleasure is something offbeat, this chapter will help you find the resources you need.

- Chapter 7, "International Travel," Leaving the country requires a new level of preparation. This chapter gives you the essentials of travel abroad.

- Chapter 8, "Healthy Travel and Special Needs," Don't let special travel needs keep you at home. Internet resources and high-tech tools can help you make travel enjoyable.

- Chapter 9, "Traveling with Pets," Can't leave Rover at the kennel? No problem. You can bring pooch or kitty along. The Internet will help you find places to stay and provide other amazing resources.

- Chapter 10, "Stay Online on the Go," Don't get out of touch. Internet cafés, laptops, hotspots, and high-tech gadgets offer many ways to stay online while you are traveling.

- Chapter 11, "Don't Leave Home without 'Em," High-tech devices can make traveling easier and more comfortable. From heated clothing to language translators, there is something for everyone.

- Chapter 12, "Sharing Memories from Your Travels," There are many new ways to share your travel experiences with others. Travel blogs, photo journals, email postcards, and other great ideas are detailed here.

My fondest wish is that you enjoy this book and let technology make your life better!

Sandy Berger

Chapter 1

The Internet: An Amazing Travel Tool

The world is a book, and those who do not travel read only a page.

—St. Augustine

The Internet is a resource that can be used for many different endeavors, but it excels as a travel tool. In fact, the Internet has almost completely reinvented the travel industry. Most of the resources that used to be available only to travel agents are now available to everyone online. This not only makes planning and executing excursions easier, but it makes planning the trip and sharing the memories with others almost as much fun as the trip itself. During the course of this book, I'll tell you about some great travel websites that will help you choose a destination, plan and execute your trip, and find bargains to make your money go further.

In This Chapter

- Travel Sites Provide Peer Reviews to Help You Learn from Others
- Travel Research Goes High-Tech

Before we begin on our journey of wonderful online travel search engines, informational websites, and bargain finders, I'd like to tell you about some Internet tools that can be fantastic helpers when you are planning to travel.

Travel Sites Provide Peer Reviews to Help You Learn from Others

About ten years ago, my husband and I took a vacation to Bermuda. We planned the trip through a reputable travel agency. The glossy brochures made the hotel look like a paradise. Travel books described the hotel property as "excellent."

When we arrived in Bermuda, reality did not support the rosy picture of the hotel. There were holes in the walls, a door without a lock, and dirt and mold everywhere. The hotel was, in our opinion, uninhabitable. We had to find other accommodations. The first day of our trip was a nightmare. We were lucky to find another hotel, or our entire vacation would have been ruined.

Fortunately, we no longer need to rely on brochures or outdated travel books. Now if a hotel is lacking in any way, guests can post their complaints, and potential visitors can read their remarks immediately. If hotel-goers are happy with their experience, they can post their praises for others to read.

Lingo

Most reputable resort or travel websites have an area for **peer reviews**, which means that they allow everyday people to post their opinions of a location or service.

Many travel websites have peer-review areas where everyday folks can post their comments. These sites have invaluable information, not only on hotels, but also on restaurants, attractions, destination locations, transportation, and tour companies. These are great places to visit before you travel to read the opinions of others. Here are just a few of the many travel sites that have areas where people can post their opinions:

- Cheap Tickets: www.cheaptickets.com

- Expedia: www.expedia.com

- Fodor's: www.fodors.com

- Frommer's: www.frommers.com

- IGoUGo: www.igougo.com

- My Travel Guide: www.mytravelguide.com

- Orbitz: www.orbitz.com

- Priceline: www.priceline.com

- Travelocity: www.travelocity.com

- TravelPost: www.travelpost.com

- Trip Advisor: www.tripadvisor.com

- VirtualTourist: www.virtualtourist.com

- Yahoo! Travel: http://travel.yahoo.com

Some websites duplicate the peer reviews found on other sites. For instance, you will find the same reviews on Orbitz as you do on Cheap Tickets. You will also find that Yahoo! Travel and Travelocity share the same reviews.

However, plenty of websites offer their own unique reviews. Several general-merchandise websites such as Epinions (www.epinions.com) now allow hotel reviews on their websites. Other unique websites such as Skytrax (www.airlinequality.com) are popping up to handle reviews of airlines and airports.

When dealing with peer reviews, you must always be careful to confirm that

BLOOPER ALERT

Be sure to judge peer-review websites with a discerning eye—don't rely too heavily one way or the other on this information. A disgruntled employee or competitor can easily post a false or misleading review. Be sure to read all the reviews. If a hotel has forty glowing reviews and one disparaging review, it may be okay to overlook that one review.

sandy's tip

Check the web-
site to see whether
the site validated that the
person posting the reviews
really used the service.

the information being posted is valid. Some websites try to prevent misleading reviews by letting
people post reviews only if they have booked their
travel through that website. Priceline and Expedia
are two such websites. Many other websites allow
anyone to post reviews with no validation that the
person posting the review ever stayed in the hotel
or ate at the restaurant, so keep that in mind as
you do your research.

To help you wade through the possible sites to choose from for peer
reviews, in the sections that follow I've highlighted four sites mentioned
in the previous list.

Frommers

Websites that have peer reviews can be very valuable for planning your
trip. For instance, after you have decided on a destination, a peer-
review area such as Frommer's busy Travel Talk Message Boards
(www.frommers.com/cgi-bin/WebX) can be useful for learning the ins
and outs of any location. They are divided into three areas. The Activity
Boards have information on beach and water sports, theme parks, winter sports, and more. The Lifestyle Boards give information on family
travel, senior travel, traveling women, and more. The Tips, Tools and
Deals Boards have information on just about everything related to
travel. The Hospitality Exchange Travel Talk board in the Tips, Tools and
Deals area even allows you to meet locals in the area where you plan to
vacation for a quick tour of the area or possibly
free place to stay.

LINGO

Message boards
are also called discus-
sion boards, bulletin boards,
and forums.

Fodors

Fodor's, another popular online travel center, also
has message boards that it calls forums at
www.fodors.com/forums. Forums include the U.S.,
Asia, Europe, and other destinations. There are

also forums for airlines, cruises, educational travel, and many others. If you visit these peer-review areas, you will find that the interface used by Fodor's is very different from many other peer-review Web areas. However, it is easy to navigate.

TripAdvisor

Another useful website that you can use to get opinions of others is the TripAdvisor (www.tripadvisor.com), as shown in Figure 1.1. This website has more than four million reviews of hotels, resorts, and vacation spots from all over the globe. You can add your own reviews and rate hotels, attractions, and restaurants. Although anyone can post a review on this website without validation, the sheer number of reviews and the large number of Web visitors makes the cream rise to the top.

The TripAdvisor site is unique because it often has a dozen or more reviews on any given hotel or restaurant. Also, you can use its Candid Photos area to get an undistorted view of what the area looks like through the camera lenses of average travelers.

This website gives you great personalized travel information, including free email newsletters. As the site has grown, it has added many new features, including goLists, where you can highlight your trips. In fact, this website is so loaded with information that it can be a bit over-whelming. Don't give up on it too easily; it has much to offer. My advice is to go through the website by clicking on the various options that you see on the front page. If you find an area you like, dig a little deeper by clicking on more links. If you happen upon an area you are not interested in, just go back to the main page and ignore that feature in the future.

sandy's tip

When you sign up for a free newsletter or register at a website, try to use an alternative email address. Sign up for a free Microsoft Live (Hotmail) email account at www.hotmail.com or for a free Yahoo! Mail account at http://mail.yahoo.com. Using these will keep any spam generated from the newsletter from infiltrating your primary email account.

FIGURE 1.1
The TripAdvisor website lists the rants and raves of everyday people about many different destinations.

VirtualTourist

The VirtualTourist website (www.virtualtourist.com), shown in Figure 1.2, takes a slightly different approach to user comments. It has information on hotels, things to do, restaurants, nightlife, and shopping, like many other websites. It also has forums where you can post comments and read the comments of others. However, when you fill out its simple sign-up form, you become a member of its virtual community. Members can post tips about any location, hotel, restaurant, shop, theater, concert, or other place or event. When you read a tip, you can rate it and/or post a comment.

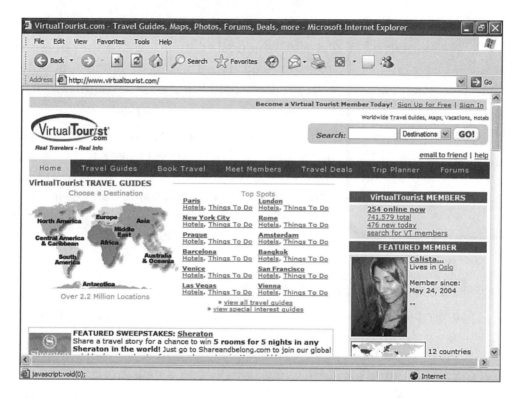

FIGURE 1.2
The VirtualTourist website lets you become a part of a virtual travel community.

VirtualTourist already has more than 700,000 members who live everywhere from New York to Singapore. Any given 24-hour period sees thousands of tips, forum postings, and comments.

At VirtualTourist you have your own email box where you can converse with other members. You are notified when others post comments on your tips. You easily see how others have rated your tips. You can create friendships and see which of your friends are online, and you can even keep track of your friends' birthdays. You can fill out a profile listing where you live, and you can add your picture. This is what makes

BLOOPER ALERT Remember not to get too personal in any online forum, message board, or email conversation. Never give out your address, telephone number, or other personal information.

the VirtualTourist fun. When you read a tip, you can see who posted it and where that person lives. You can respond with your comments, and if you like, you can email the person for additional information.

While you can create your own VirtualTourist home page and build travel pages to trace your wanderings, the true beauty of the website is in its community. Active participants can get a lot of information not just from travelers, but also from locals who live all over the world.

Travel Research Goes High-Tech

You probably know that the Internet is a wonderful tool for travel planning. First, though, I'd like to tell you about some of the new, free Internet tools that can bring travel information to your desktop quickly and easily. From electronic newsletters and emails to RSS feeds and blogs, there's virtually no limit to ways you can find information. Don't worry if these terms sound like something from *Star Trek* to you right now. Soon you'll see how to make the Internet do your travel research for you using these very tools.

Electronic Newsletters

It's always fun to think about your next vacation, even if you just came back from one. It can be exciting to get travel newsletters that can give you destination ideas or transport you to another location, even if only in your mind. Electronic newsletters are popular and easy to find. Just surf to your favorite travel website and look for a link to sign up for its newsletter. Many of these newsletters are free, and most prominently advertise that there is no cost involved for the end user.

Some travel sites offer you their free newsletter without any information or examples. If you like the website, don't hesitate to try its newsletter.

Some sites show you examples of the newsletter or list topics that are included, which is even better. An example is the AARP Travel Newsletter, which can be previewed at www.aarp.org/emailnews_preview?newsletter=travel.

The best, however, is when a website displays its current newsletter right on the site and archives all the old newsletters online as well. With this setup, you can be pleasantly surprised to see the newsletter announcement when it arrives in your inbox and you can read the newsletter immediately, if you like. Later you can easily find any or all of the newsletters online, so you can continue to have access to them at any time without having to rummage through old email to find them. Frommer's newsletter at www.frommers.com/newsletters is a good example of a newsletter that is available online. Another example is Elliott's Email Travel letter at http://www.elliott.org/vault/newsletter.

Newsletters often give you an edge in finding travel discounts and special promotions that you might not find out about otherwise. For instance, the *Seattle Times* at http://seattletimes.nwsource.com/html/traveloutdoors will send you travel promotions and deals once a month or whenever they become available. SmarterTravel (www.smartertravel.com) has a newsletter that is filled with travel deals and advice.

Most major airlines will send you a weekly email with their special offers and sales. Here are a few:

- American Airlines' Sale Alert: www.aa.com
- Southwest Airlines' Click 'n Save Specials: www.southwest.com/hotfares
- US Airways' E-Savers: www.usairways.comokay
- United's E-Fares: www.ual.comokay

As you surf the Internet on your quest for travel information, keep an eye out for newsletters that are geared toward specific interests you may have. For instance, if you are an RVer, you may want to subscribe to the RVtravel.com newsletter at www.rvtravel.com. If you are going to London, you will find that the BBC has a London Travel Newsletter (www.bbc.co.uk/london/travel/newsletter/newsletter.shtml), as shown in Figure 1.3, which is sure to provide interesting information.

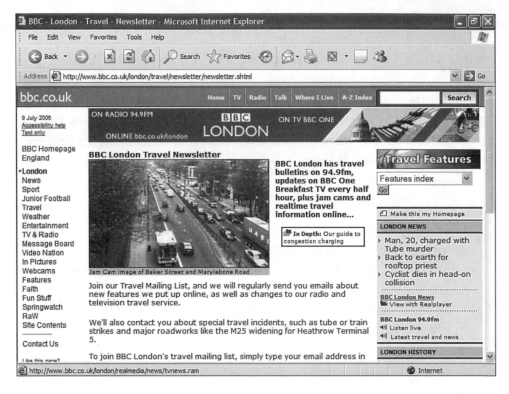

FIGURE 1.3
The BBC London Travel Newsletter can be invaluable for planning a trip to London.

Although most of the newsletters I've mentioned are free, if you travel a lot, it may be worthwhile to subscribe to one or two travel newsletters, even if you have to pay for them. The First Class Flyer newsletter (www.firstclassflyer.com) that I subscribe to has given me information on everything from getting the most comfortable airline seats to saving money on flights.

Email Alerts

Similar to electronic newsletters that provide you with travel information and links to other resources, you can sign up for email notifications to get instant access to travel deals and information on special promotions. Unlike newsletters, which usually come once a week or once a month, alerts can be sent at any time. Besides offering bargains and deals, email alerts can also be very useful for a variety of other information, such as travel advisories and flight information.

Many hotels offer email alerts. Here are some popular ones to check out:

- Hyatt: www.hyatt.com
- Radisson: www.radisson.com/hotdeals
- Holiday Inn: www.basshotels.com/holiday-inn
- Best Western: www.bestwestern.com
- Hilton: www.hilton.com

When looking for email alerts, don't miss the airline sites. If you sign up for the United Airlines email program, you can get messages about electronic fare offers as well as email about your Mileage Plus account.

Some alerts are like a newsletter, with graphics and complete articles. Others are simply one- or two-line alerts with timely information.

The New York Times Travel Deals by email (http://travel.nytimes.com/pages/travel/index.htm) is somewhere in the middle. It lists timely travel offers from the *New York Times'* newspaper advertisers. You can see a sample of the email alert (see Figure 1.4) by clicking the "See Sample" link in the Travel Deals by Email box on the main page. It looks a little like a newsletter with good formatting and nice images. Yet, it has blurbs of information on travel deals. You can click the links if you want more information.

FIGURE 1.4

The New York Times Great Getaways email alert has pictures and brief explanations of their many bargains.

At Smartraveller (www.smartraveller.com), which is an Australian government website, you can sign up to be notified by email when a travel advisory is posted for any country.

Some airline websites go even further than email notifications. American Airlines will send flight departure/arrival and gate information to your home phone, mobile phone, pager, or personal digital assistant, as well as by email.

A look around the Web will turn up many other useful email notifications that you can subscribe to.

RSS Feeds

A great way to get travel information on the Internet is by RSS (Really Simple Syndication) feed. When a website that supports RSS posts new articles and you subscribe to its RSS service, a list of titles of the new content, along with a link to the complete article, appear automatically in your RSS news aggregator program.

A website that has the RSS service available generally announces this on its main page and/or has a small orange rectangular button marked either XML or RSS somewhere on the page, as shown in Figure 1.5. Most people try to click this button. In many cases, clicking it just gives you a page of computer code that looks like gobbledygook, or you may get a confusing page asking you to choose the news aggregator you are using.

> ## LINGO
>
> **RSS (Really Simple Syndication)** is a type of news aggregation that feeds headlines and links to new stories to the end user automatically.

> ## LINGO
>
> A **news aggregator** is a program that handles RSS feeds and makes them appear in that program automatically. Many Web browsers now can act as RSS news aggregator programs.

You need an RSS newsreader to find, accumulate, and present the RSS information. Several good newsreaders are available for Windows users. FeedDemon (www.newsgator.com) and SharpReader (www.sharpreader.net) are two of them. Excellent choices for Mac users are NetNewsWire (www.newsgator.com) and Six Apart (www.sixapart.com). Some newsreaders like Bloglines (www.bloglines.com) have versions for both PC and Mac. Many of these readers are free, but each requires a learning curve to use them.

There is an easier way to subscribe to an RSS news feed. Simply use a Web browser that supports RSS feeds. The Firefox Web browser, which is available at www.firefox.com, supports them, as does the Opera Web browser, which is available at www.opera.com.

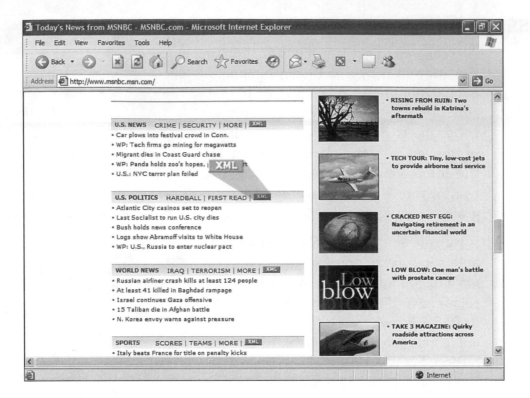

FIGURE 1.5
An orange rectangle with the letters XML or RSS indicates that the website you are viewing provides RSS news feeds.

sandy's tip
If you decide to upgrade to Internet Explorer 7, you will be pleased to find other features such as tabbed browsing and the ability to make websites appear larger on the screen and to print better than in previous versions.

If you are using Internet Explorer 6 as your Web browser and you don't want to go to the trouble of changing to a new browser, you can simply surf to the Microsoft website at www.microsoft.com/windows/ie and download the newer version, Version 7, which supports RSS feeds.

If you have a Web browser that is RSS-enabled, you see a square orange button near the top of the screen that indicates that the browser can act as a news aggregator. In Internet Explorer 7, it appears on the right side near the top of the screen, as shown in Figure 1.6. In the Firefox and

Opera Web browsers, it appears on the right side of the address bar, as shown in Figure 1.7.

FIGURE 1.6
In Internet Explorer 7, when a Web page has RSS feeds available, the RSS icon appears near the top of the screen.

FIGURE 1.7
In Firefox, when you visit a website that has an RSS feed, you see an orange button on the address bar.

When you find an interesting website and you want to subscribe to its RSS feed, you simply click the RSS button in your browser. Another window may appear, giving you information about the RSS information from this website. Just click "Subscribe," and you're done.

Your browser then collects all the current news stories from the website you chose. It does this automatically in the background without your having to do a thing.

Each Web browser handles RSS feeds slightly differently. When you are ready to look at the list of new stories, how you access them depends on which browser you are using.

It is very easy to access your RSS lists if you are using Internet Explorer 7. Just click the star on the left side of the screen, as shown in Figure 1.8. Then click the Feeds button. A list of the RSS feeds you have subscribed to appears. Choose the one you want to see. A list of stories appears with the news headlines and links to the full story.

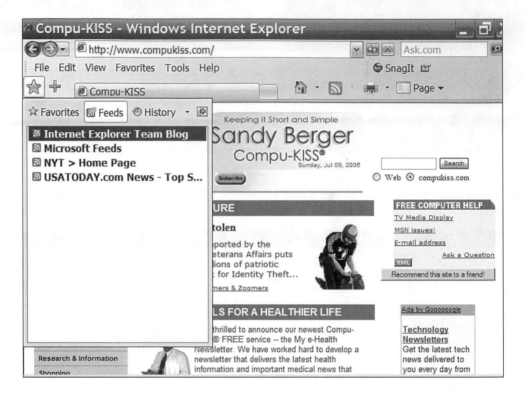

FIGURE 1.8
In Internet Explorer 7, it is easy to access the RSS feeds you have subscribed to.

The Firefox Web browser puts the RSS feeds in the Bookmarks Toolbar folder. You can access them through the Bookmarks menu option. The Opera Web browser has a Feeds choice on the main menu that you can use to look at your RSS information.

Using RSS feeds is convenient, and it can be fun as well. You will find many travel websites that have RSS feeds. Here are a few to get you started:

- Frommer's: www.frommers.com
- *New York Times*: http://travel.nytimes.com/pages/travel
- *USA Today*: www.usatoday.com/travel

■ *Minneapolis Star-Tribune:* www. startribune.com/travel

■ *Philadelphia Daily News:* www. philly.com/travel

Don't forget that you can use RSS feeds for current news as well as travel news.

Podcasts

Every now and then a new technology fad that is truly useful appears on the scene. Podcasting is one of these. It started as a high-tech craze and now has caught on with millions of everyday people who find it both fun and useful. It is especially popular and valuable for finding travel information.

Podcasting is a new method of distributing audio programming. A podcast is special broadcast content that is distributed over the Internet. "Podcast" is a combination of "iPod" and "broadcast." The word itself is a little misleading, because although you can listen to podcasts with an iPod or other digital music players, you don't have to own a portable player to listen to a podcast. You can listen over the Internet using your computer. You can also install software that automatically downloads every instance of any show(s) you choose. Then you can listen on your computer at your convenience or download the shows to your music player for added portability.

Listening to travel podcasts is much like sitting around the kitchen table listening to friends tell you about their travels. But in this case, the friends can be friendly travel experts who are sharing not only travel experience, but also useful tips and money-saving advice. Also, you don't have to gather in the kitchen or living room on

LINGO

Podcasts are radio-style audio files that are transmitted over the Internet. They can be listened to on a computer or transferred to a digital music player for portable listening.

BLOOPER ALERT

Many people think you need an iPod to listen to podcasts. You don't. You can listen to them on your computer.

a Saturday evening to hear a podcast. You can listen to podcasts anytime on your computer and anytime and anywhere on a portable MP3 player.

Podcasts are recurring events, like a television series or a daily radio show. Podcasts can be created daily, weekly, monthly, or at any interval that the podcast creator decides on. If you have a portable MP3 player, you can also download the podcast to the player, just as you would transfer a song.

Podcasts can be developed by those who are willing to add some audio hardware and software to their computers and take the time to record audio programming. This has opened the world of traditional radio-type broadcasting to a new type of enthusiast, resulting in thousands of different podcasts. Most podcasts are geared to a specific topic and are produced for a special audience. You can find podcasts on mountain climbing, wine tasting, baseball, movies, and, of course, travel. In fact, since people love to talk about their travel experiences, travel is a natural fit for podcasters.

Podcasts can help travelers choose a destination, plan their trip, and budget their money. Any website that has podcasts will have a way to listen to them on your computer by simply clicking a link to the podcast. A window pops up, and the audio starts. (You may be asked to download an audio player, but your computer probably already has all the software you need.)

You can bookmark the podcast page in your Web browser so that you can easily come back later to see if a new podcast has been posted. You can "subscribe" to a podcast by using a free software program that automatically downloads every new episode of any podcast that you have subscribed to. Apple's iTunes is the most popular software for downloading and playing music, and it is also the most popular podcast software.

Sandy's tip
Although downloading music with iTunes costs money, almost all the podcasts are free.

For further information on podcasts and how iTunes works, be sure to visit my Compu-KISS website at www.compukiss.com.

Listening to podcasts is more relaxing than reading text on the computer screen. When you are tired of reading and ready to give your ears a workout, here are a couple of travel podcasts I think you'll enjoy:

- The Lonely Planet Travelcasts area at www.lonelyplanet.com/podcasts has podcasts that let you listen to experts talk about travel.

- The Discovery Channel podcasts at www.discovery.com/radio/podcasts.html#travelchannel talk about everything from the ski patrol on Canada's Mt. Whistlet to icy summer treats in hot Southern cities.

You can find more podcasts on travel, as well as other topics, by downloading the free Apple iTunes software at www.itunes.com and visiting the iTunes Music Store.

More travel podcasts can be found at the Digital Podcast website at www.digitalpodcast.com/browse-travel-31-1.html. The first page of listings is shown in Figure 1.9. Be patient. You'll find about twelve such pages of travel podcasts here.

You'll find that the Digital Podcast website has podcasts for many different travel areas of interest. The Las Vegas Insider Podcast is perfect if you are planning a trip to the fantasy city. General Aviation Weekly is great for flying enthusiasts. There is also the Trip to Tuscany podcast, plus much more. Although some of the podcasts are targeted at certain travel destinations, many are more general in nature, such as the Amateur Traveler, the Connected Traveler, and Red Eye Radio.

To give you an idea of just how many travel podcasts there are to choose from, I can tell you that Richard Branson, renowned travel addict and CEO of Virgin Atlantic airlines, has downloaded more than 200,000 podcasts in less than a year from their online site (www.virgin-atlantic.com) and from Apple's iTunes store for destinations ranging from Shanghai to Las Vegas.

FIGURE 1.9
The Digital Podcast website has extensive listings of travel podcasts.

You may find that listening to travel podcasts is your cup of tea. When you listen to others talk about their travel adventures, you are sure to get ideas for your own as well.

LINGO

A *blog* is a personal journal that is posted on the Web. The word "blog" comes from "Web log."

Blogs

Blogs are listings of thoughts and ideas by one author or a group of authors. On many blogs, after the blog creator has posted his thoughts and comments, anyone can post a comment on his post. On other blogs, you can only read the blog entries—you can't post comments.

Like message boards, blogs are usually confined to a given topic. For instance, on the Ship to Shore blog at SmarterTravel.com (www. smartertravel.com/blogs/ship-to-shore), editor Erica Silverstein reports on the latest cruise-industry news. As shown in Figure 1.10, at this blog you see a list of current postings with a link to read the entire article. You cannot post comments on this blog.

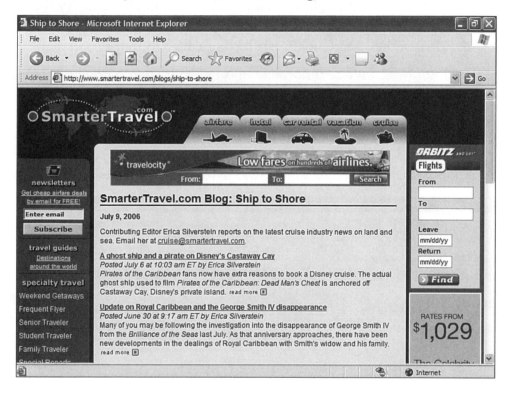

FIGURE 1.10
The SmarterTravel.com Ship to Shore blog reports on the latest cruise-industry news.

SmarterTravel.com has several different blogs where its travel experts post current news as well as personal comments. Their Destination Watch blog follows destination trends and offers destination warnings. The Today in Travel blog reports on news that affects travelers, and the Up Front blog deals with flight issues.

How to Find Travel Blogs

To find a wide variety of travel blogs, visit TravelBlog at www.travelblog.org. You can read the blogs, which they sometimes call journals, of others who have visited many different countries. At TravelBlog anyone can add comments to another's blog.

If you are looking for a blog on a certain travel destination, try the Google Blog Search engine located at http://blogsearch.google.com. Just type in the destination, and Google lists blogs related to that destination.

Technorati at www.technorati.com is another search engine created just for finding blogs on the topic of your choice. You can use Technorati just as you would use Google—by entering the type of blog you are looking for and getting a list of results. You can also go directly to its travel blog area at www.technorati.com/blogs/travel. As shown in Figure 1.11, the Technorati Blog Finder has extensive listings of travel blogs.

FIGURE 1.11
The Technorati Blog Finder has many listings under Travel.

Create Your Own Travel Blog

Have ever wished that you had kept a journal of your travels? TravelBlog gives you a chance to create a travel blog of your own. It lets you create a blog (journal) of as many trips as you like. You can add photos and routes and even automatically notify your friends and family when you add something to your blog. You can even pinpoint on a map all the states and/or countries that you have visited. It's all free, and it's one of the easiest ways to start blogging.

If you are interested in starting your own travel blog, you will also want to visit TravelPod.com at www.travelpod.com. This is another website that allows you to create your own blog and share your travel adventures with your friends. Like TravelBlog, TravelPod is free and lets you create maps and post photos.

sandy's tip

You can blog while you travel. Just stop at any Internet café or wireless hot spot and add your day's travel notes and comments to your blog. You will not only get to document your trips and share your travels with others, but you may find that you are a talented travel journalist.

Webcams

Reading the accounts of others and getting news from experts can be very beneficial, but there is nothing like seeing a place with your own eyes. The Internet lets you do that by using webcams. These Internet-connected cameras are located all over the world. They show you what is happening as it happens. You can watch the skiers in Zermatt, Switzerland or view a street corner in London.

Webcams are not only great for checking out a future destination, but when you just can't get away, they let you do a little "armchair" traveling.

LINGO

A **webcam** is a camera that lets you view live images over the Internet.

You can find webcams with a simple search engine such as Google (www.google.com). Entering the words *webcam Zermatt* gave me listing of six websites with webcams of Zermatt. Entering *webcam London* gave me listings of webcams all over London.

If you just want to see how many webcams are available and perhaps experience a few of them, visit the EarthCam website at www.earthcam.com. It's not quite like being there, but it's fun to see the ships sail by in front of the Statue of Liberty, the view from the Space Needle in Seattle, and people on the beach in St. Thomas.

Sandy's Summary

The Internet and other high-tech tools have changed the entire travel industry. Today the Internet can help you plan and execute your trip, making it more fun than ever before.

Peer-review sites ensure that you vacation in a great area, stay at a good hotel, and make the best travel accommodations possible.

Travel newsletters and email alerts keep you up-to-date on travel news and make you aware of bargains that are available to make your trip more affordable.

RSS feeds do even more to keep you up-to-date. You can subscribe to your favorite RSS travel website. Every time that site posts new articles, the information is automatically transferred to your RSS news aggregator. RSS feeds used to be the playground of only highly technical people, but today's Web browsers make them easy for everyone to use.

Blogs are a way for you to keep up with other people's travels, and you can easily create your own. In the travel world, blogs act as travel logs or journals. Creating one with today's wonderful tools is both fun and easy.

Webcams let you see live happenings from all over the world. You can view people on a beach, see skiers enjoying their sport, or just watch people crossing the street halfway around the world.

Yes, the Internet and other high-tech tools are making travel and travel planning more fun than ever before.

Sandy Berger

Chapter 2

Planning Your Trip

*I travel not to go anywhere, but to go. I travel for travel's sake.
The great affair is to move.*

—Robert Louis Stevenson

So you've decided to take a trip. Where do you start with your planning? The Internet, of course. That's where you can get ideas on where to go and what to see. It's where you can check the weather and find local events, hotels, and restaurants. On the Internet you can see what the experts think, and you can also get the opinions of regular travelers just like you. You can even create your own travel guide. Whether you are thinking of visiting the battlefields of Gettysburg or taking a horseback tour in Mongolia, the Internet will help you plan and execute your trip.

Researching Your Destination

The Internet puts information about every destination in the world at your fingertips. It makes you realize just how much there is to see and do in the world. Whether you are a globetrotter or you like to stick closer to home, your questions are often the same. Where should I go? What should I see?

Don't worry. Although you have a myriad of choices, the Internet can help you sort it all out.

Tourism Websites

A great place to start is with tourism websites. These are unique websites that were created specifically to showcase a particular area of the country or world.

Every state in the U.S. has its own website. Each can be found at www.state.*XX*.us, where *XX* is the state's abbreviation. For example, the official state website of Illinois is www.state.il.us. You can often find interesting information that relates to travel at these websites. For instance, the Illinois website has weather information, road construction status, and gasoline prices. It also has information about hunting and fishing licenses.

At the each state website you can find links to the tourist area. Unfortunately, each state's tourist website name has a different format. For instance, New York is http://iloveny.com, and Maryland is www. mdisfun.org. Here are a few others:

- Arizona: www.arizonaguide.com
- California: http://gocalif.ca.gov
- Florida: www.gofloridavacations.com
- Hawaii: www.visit.hawaii.org
- Indiana: www.enjoyindiana.com
- Minnesota: www.exploreminnesota.com
- South Carolina: www.discoversouthcarolina.com
- Tennessee: www.tnvacation.com
- Virginia: www.Virginia.org
- Wisconsin: www.travelwisconsin.com

As you can see, you can't guess the Web addresses for most of the state tourism offices. An easy way to find the tourism office for each state is to use the Tourism Offices Worldwide Directory at www.towd. com. As shown in Figure 2.1, it has links to the tourism offices in the various states, as well as those for other countries. It even has a list of the most frequently requested destinations each week.

FIGURE 2.1
The Tourism Offices Worldwide Directory is a wonderful resource for finding tourism websites.

Today every state and many countries have tourism websites that list attractions, accommodations, restaurants, and local activities. They often have information on traveling to their location as well.

The Tourism Offices Worldwide Directory lists many of the world's most popular destinations. If the area you are interested in is not listed, you can probably find it by using any search engine. Just enter the area's name followed by the word *tourism*. For example, Aruba is not

Sandy's tip

Although each search engine gives similar results, they are not all exactly the same. So it is often advantageous to use several different search engines to get the most possible results.

listed in the directory. So you would go to Google at www.google.com and type in *Aruba tourism*. The first result is Aruba's official tourism website, www.aruba.com. Other search engines, such as Windows Live at www.live.com and Ask.com at www.ask.com, will produce similar results.

Another great website for tourism links is 123World at www.123world.com/tourism. This site has links to official tourism websites of many countries and geographic regions. You must scroll down the screen to the alphabetical listings. There you will find links to a large number of countries, states, and areas, as shown in Figure 2.2.

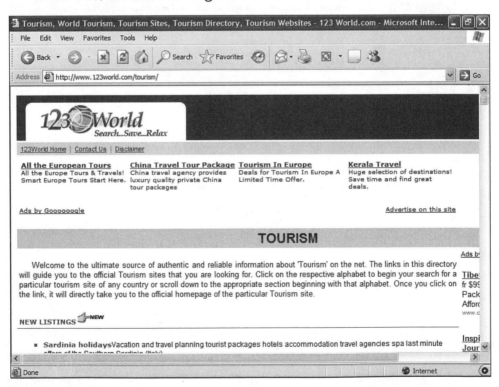

FIGURE 2.2

The 123World website has an extensive list of links to official tourism websites of different countries, regions, and states.

Concierge.com

All of this is very helpful if you have some idea of where you want to go. But what if you want to try something different and you don't have a clue as to where you want to go or what you want to do?

Try a website like the online home of Conde Nast Traveler, which is called Concierge.com (www.concierge.com). A quick visit gives you a wealth of great choices. The Ideas section, shown in Figure 2.3, has a Destination finder that gives you vacation ideas. Just choose from categories such as adventure, beach, culinary, cultural, family, gold, luxury, romantic, and skiing. Then choose an area of the world and the time of year you might want to travel. You are presented with ideas and a destination guide for each.

FIGURE 2.3
The Ideas area of the Concierge.com website will start you on your way to a fun-filled vacation.

BLOOPER ALERT

Always be sure to type Internet addresses exactly as they are given. Typing www.fromers.com instead of www.frommers. com will lead you to a different travel website.

Frommers.com

Frommer's, a company known for its travel guides, also has a Web presence that can give you a multitude of trip ideas. Just select Trip Ideas from the Frommer's menu at www.frommers.com.

In 1957 the first Frommer's book, *Europe on $5 a Day*, was published. Maybe you even used it for a youthful tour of Europe. Now Frommer's publishes more than 300 travel guidebooks. Some of its books have been updated many times. The current *$ a Day* book for Europe is in its 46th edition. Not surprisingly, this edition is called *Europe from $85 a Day*.

With all that travel guidebook experience, it is not surprising that Frommer's has an excellent website. Under trip ideas are sections for disabled, family, gay and lesbian, honeymoon, senior, single, student, and women. Ideas are also listed by activities, such as beach and water sports, cruise, outdoor and adventure, road trip, theme park, and winter sport.

The Frommer's site is sure to give you some trip ideas. Its Calendar Of Events (www.frommers.com/tips/calendar_of_events) contains events to suit a wide range of tastes. It lists everything from a rip-roaring Rattlesnake Roundup festival and parade in Sweetwater, Texas to a classy Oxford and Cambridge collegiate boat race in London, England.

The Frommer's site also offers helpful printable trip planners. If you like to be organized, the printable activity planners will keep you on track as well.

Destination Ideas

If you lack inspiration for trip ideas, the SoGoNow website at www.SoGoNow.com, shown in Figure 2.4, may be the answer. Many other travel sites help you find airfares and hotel rooms, but the SoGoNow site is dedicated to providing travelers with inspiration for their vacations. This site has thousands of vacation ideas, travel articles, travel news, and forums. Although it is filled with ads, it also has much information and may give you the idea that will become your next great adventure.

FIGURE 2.4
The SoGoNow website features special vacation ideas and destinations.

Still haven't found a destination to your liking? Don't worry; there are plenty of other places to look for ideas. Lonely Planet at www.lonelyplanet.com gives you solid information on just about every country in the world. You won't find small towns or villages, but many large cities are represented. Although this site doesn't have a destination guide, you can choose any country or large city and get useful travel information. An overview of the area includes background information, weather, culture and history, median hotel and meal prices, places to see, and even information on how to get there. The Lonely Planet website also gives information on recent weather devastations, disease outbreaks, political upheavals, and other conditions that may affect travel to that area.

You can also get information and destination ideas by checking the travel features at the Lonely Planet Travel Feature area, www.lonelyplanet.com/journeys. This area has news and features that can be chosen by region or author.

As shown in Figure 2.5, Don George, the site's travel expert, has his own area at www.lonelyplanet.com/journeys/wwdgd. He posts articles regularly, and you can ask him a question and read the questions that others have asked.

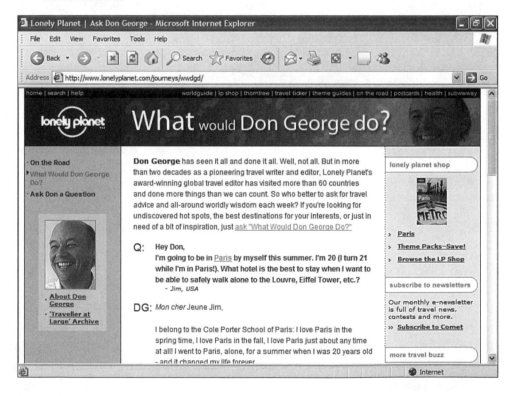

FIGURE 2.5
Don George, travel expert, has a "What Would Don George Do?" area at the Lonely Planet website.

Start Planning

After you settle on a destination, plenty of online information can help you with your trip planning, including travel services, accommodations, and activities.

If you were planning a trip twenty years ago, your first destination would be to a bookstore or library, where you could pick up some travel guides. Vacationers have relied on guidebooks to plan trips for many years. Yet, because of the high cost of printing, publishers create books for only the most popular destinations. Also, the wealth of information on the Internet far surpasses any guidebook. As a matter of fact, you can use the Internet to create your own guidebook, complete with news, local events, and weather reports that will be more current than anything you can find in a book.

Why not start at the website of the granddaddy of all travel guides—the Fodor's website at www.fodors.com?

Of course, the Fodor's site tries to sell you its guidebooks, but it also has plenty of free information. When you pick a destination, you get an overview of the area, advice on when to go, shopping, hotel, sights, and activities. The great thing about this website is that it is interactive. The restaurants are rated by website visitors; after you visit, you can add your own review. While you are at the Fodor's website, be sure to select *Talk* from the main menu, as shown in Figure 2.6. This takes you to the travel talk forums, where you can read trip reports and advice from Fodor's many Web visitors.

Fodor's is a comprehensive travel site. Click any destination to get an overview along with a descriptive picture. The left menu bar has specific information about the place you chose. These links vary depending on the destination you are viewing, but they usually include information about restaurants, hotels, sights and activities, side trips, nightlife and arts, and shopping. Most destinations also have Smart Travel tips, which include information about getting to that area, getting around while you are there, and additional contacts and resources.

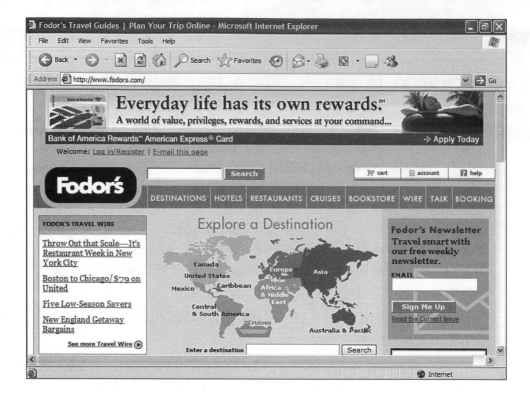

FIGURE 2.6
Select Talk from the menu at Fodor's website to learn about and from the experiences of others.

The *When to Go* link gives you the most popular times to visit and tells you why those times are so well-liked. The Fodor's site also has an excellent National Parks guide (www.fodors.com/parks) that has information about all U.S. and Canadian national parks.

Although the Fodor's website is filled with great information and covers many popular destinations, many places are not included. For instance, in the entire state of Wisconsin, only Milwaukee is listed. Seven areas are listed for North Carolina, but my hometown of Pinehurst, a very popular tourist destination, is not included.

This means that you might want to check out a few more websites to find out more about the destination you've chosen. Let's look at another website that developed around travel guides—the Frommer's website at www.frommers.com. We just looked at it for destination ideas, but it is also a great guide after you have decided on a vacation spot. Click the Destinations tab at the Frommer's website to get more information on the place you've chosen.

The Frommer's site's city guides aren't limited to big cities. You can find brief information about even small and medium-sized cities, including hotels and restaurants, attractions, and side trips. Bigger cities typically have much more information, including histories, descriptions of neighborhoods, and suggested walking tours, but it's nice to be able to find some information about small towns. My hometown of Pinehurst is mentioned here.

In addition to cities, the Destinations section lets you see the highlights of wider regions, such as "outside L.A." and "the I-40 corridor."

For another great guide to possible destinations, try the Yahoo! Travel website at http://travel.yahoo.com. I find the main page of this site pretty mundane. You can search for flights, hotels, cars, and cruises, just as you can at many other travel websites. All these functions are useful, but I find the Yahoo! Travel Guide area (http://travel.yahoo.com/travelguide) unique and exciting. It is one of my favorites because it has so much easy-to-access information.

You must have a Yahoo! account to access the full power of the trip planner. Just fill in the short sign-up form to get a username and password. Then log in and click the Travel Guides tab, as shown in Figure 2.7.

You are taken to an area overflowing with places to visit and sights to see. This area has lists of hotels, things to do, restaurants, shopping, and entertainment. You can browse through 500,000 places to stay and things to do in more than 40,000 cities.

Click trip plan or surf to http://travel.yahoo.com/trip to begin your online journey. Then you simply enter your proposed trip destination and travel dates. You are presented with a list of hotels, things to do, restaurants, shopping, and entertainment that will be available in the city of your choice during the time of your stay.

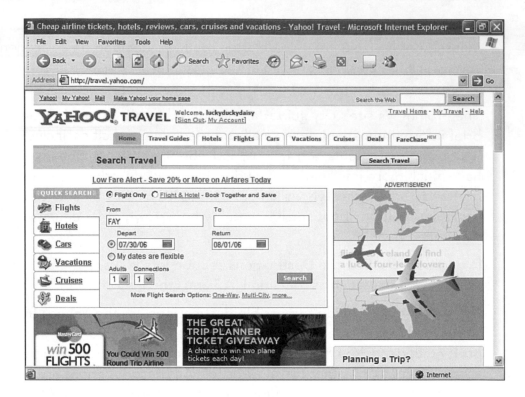

FIGURE 2.7
The Yahoo! Travel Guides will help you plan your perfect trip.

Each section (such as hotels or restaurants) has its own area. Suppose you decide on a trip to Chicago for the beginning of July. Click Hotels, and you get a list of hotels along with a rating and the average price. These can be sorted alphabetically, by popularity, or by price. Clicking any hotel gives you the location, map, hotel class, user reviews, photos, and amenities. You also get a useful list of nearby restaurants and things to do in the hotel's area.

Of course, you can make a reservation, look at other hotels, or simply add the hotel to your trip as a possibility.

The Yahoo! Trip Planner is impressive in its scope. For instance, it knows that the *Oprah Winfrey Show* is taping during your proposed stay and that the Taste of Chicago and fireworks display will also be held at that time. It tells you how to get tickets to *Oprah* and gives you a link where you can get all the information you need about the Taste, Chicago's biggest street fair.

If you want to go to the Museum of Natural History in Chicago, Yahoo! gives you a write-up on the museum, its address and telephone number, hours of operation, cost, a map showing the location, and a link to the museum's website.

Another website called My Travel Guide, at www.mytravelguide.com, provides a trip-planning service similar to Yahoo! Travel (see Figure 2.8). This site also requires that you fill out a short form and get a username and password to access its trip planning.

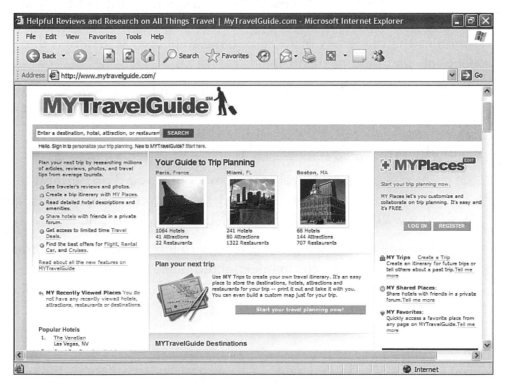

FIGURE 2.8
The My Travel Guide website helps you plan your next trip.

BLOOPER ALERT
When you sign up, often there is a check box that says "Send me special travel deals" or something similar. Be sure to remove the check mark if you don't want the extra mailings.

Although this site has plenty of information, the interface used for the trip planning is more difficult to navigate than Yahoo!. If you try it and find it a bit too complicated, remember that this site is still a good place for checking ratings of hotels, restaurants, and attractions, because the listings are comprehensive. For instance, it rates and gives information on more than 700 hotels in London and more than 1,200 restaurants in Atlanta.

When you are dealing with online resources, information about travel can come from some unusual sources. For instance, you might not think of your alumni association when you are planning your travel, yet some schools, such as the University of Arizona, have an alumni association that actively helps alums plan trips.

The University of Arizona Alumni Association has its own travel website (www.arizonaalumni.com/Travel). As shown in Figure 2.9, it says, "It's not just where...but with whom..." It lets you book travel with old friends and others who might have similar interests.

Schools may be good travel resources even if you didn't attend that school. For instance, Duke University has an excellent travel research area at www.lib.duke.edu/reference/subjects/travel.html.

So when you are planning a trip, it pays to look around online. You may find wonderful resources in unexpected places.

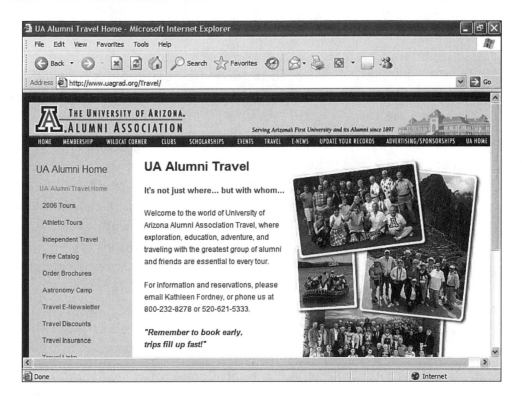

FIGURE 2.9
There are many unusual places to look for travel information. If you attended the University of Arizona, you can travel with your classmates.

More Online Planning Resources

Online media outlets are great places to look for travel information. You might already be aware of sites hosted by the Travel Channel and MSNBC, but are you aware that resources such as newspapers and magazines have gone high-tech and provide access to information 24/7? These days even small local newspapers have their own websites. Don't miss this fantastic resource for choosing a destination or planning a trip.

Electronic Newspapers

Newspapers have always been a part of the travel scene. Many papers have weekly sections devoted to travel that can provide you with a hometown view of a travel destination that you might not get looking at major travel sites.

Instead of using a search engine or looking through online newspapers, a great place to get links to the travel sections of many newspapers is TripSpot at www.tripspot.com/newspapers.htm. All the major newspapers that have travel sections are listed here; you just click to peruse one of the publications. While you are at the TripSpot newspaper area, you may want to click the home button, which takes you to www.tripspot.com. It has an extensive travel area, with sections on Getting There, Where to Stay, What to Do, and a Travel Library.

If you want to access a good newspaper travel section directly, the *USA Today* Travel area at www.usatoday.com/travel is a great place to start. Its travel area has news, photos, hotels, an airfare search, and a specials and deals area. For general travel information, the *USA Today* site has eight travel columnists who cover everything from hotel and airport reviews to business travel. For your planning, it has a Destination area, as shown in Figure 2.10. This area is filled with destination ideas, city guides, and news.

Like the *USA Today* Travel area, the *New York Times* Travel site has ongoing articles by noted travel journalists. Like many other travel sites, it has deals, booking, and travel guides. The Escapes area at www.nytimes.com/pages/travel/escapes, however, is somewhat unique. It gives information on short getaways for North American cities. A new city is added each week. Each review includes an itinerary that provides details such as places to eat and sights to see. Telephone numbers are given for each place so that you can check availability and make a speedy reservation. In today's fast-paced world, it's nice to have a quick weekend trip already planned for you. These provide no-brainer mini-vacations with the planning already done.

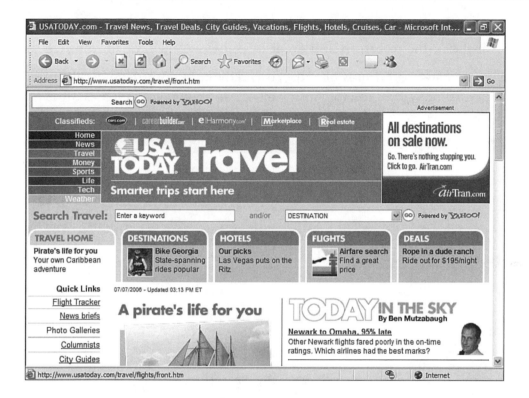

FIGURE 2.10
USA Today's website has an area dedicated to destinations.

The *New York Times* Travel area also gives you a list of the articles that its Web visitors have emailed the most to their friends and the articles that have been most popular with bloggers.

Online newspapers may also be a good resource if you will be traveling to the city that hosts the newspaper. For instance, the *Boston Globe's* Travel area at www.boston.com/travel has a Boston Visitors' Guide section that is very informative.

The *Chicago Tribune's* travel area at www.chicagotribune.com/travel has an area called Midwest Travel that features travel information for Illinois, Indiana, Iowa, Michigan, Minnesota, Missouri, Ohio, and Wisconsin.

The *Milwaukee Journal Sentinel* has tons of information on Wisconsin-related things to see and do at http://www.onwisconsin.com/travel.

The *New York Times* at http://travel.nytimes.com/pages/travel has an excellent guide to Northern Ireland, as shown in Figure 2.11. It is filled with things to do and "don't miss" places in Northern Ireland.

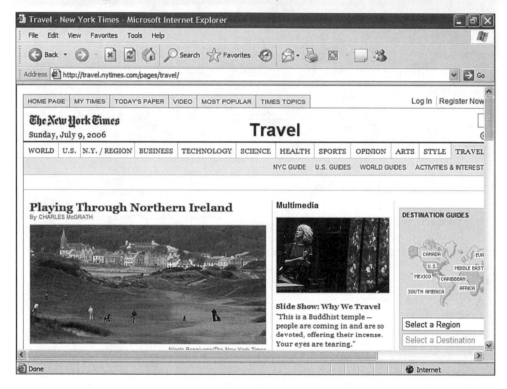

FIGURE 2.11
The *New York Times* has an excellent travel guide to Northern Ireland.

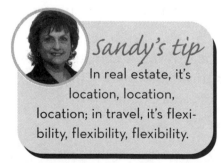

Sandy's tip
In real estate, it's location, location, location; in travel, it's flexibility, flexibility, flexibility.

So be sure to check out the local papers online while you are doing your vacation planning.

Electronic Travel Magazines

TimeOut magazine (www.timeout.com) has an online arm that is excellent for trip planning. As you might expect from a magazine-oriented website, the travel features and articles are excellent. What you might not expect is the extensive list of cities around the world. The list begins with Abu Dhabi and ends with Zurich. Many wonderful places are listed in between. Just click any city, and you are presented with an overview and an online city guide that includes sightseeing, restaurants, nightlife, shopping, and hotels.

Travel & Leisure Magazine (www.travelandleisure.com) also has excellent online information, which includes the current month's issue, restaurants, and hot deals.

Also, be sure to visit the *National Geographic Traveler* magazine (www. nationalgeographic.com/traveler). While you may think of National Geographic covering only exotic destinations, you will find that this online magazine covers destinations such as Milwaukee, Wisconsin and the Bahamas. Like its paper counterpart, the website also has wonderful photos, including a photo of the week which you can download and use as you computer monitor's background (wallpaper) .

MSNBC and the Travel Channel

Another great travel website from a media-oriented company is the MSNBC Travel area. You get there by selecting the Travel menu choice at the MSNBC website at www.msnbc.msn.com (see Figure 2.12). After you access the Travel area, you can select the Destination menu choice for some wonderful destination ideas. Expect to spend some time at the MSNBC Travel site, because there is much to explore, including road trips, gold travel, family travel, travel tips, and more. The MSNBC site has an area where you can sound off about your bad trips. It also has an interesting area called "24-Hour Layover" where you can get many ideas for a quick visit to many different cities, including Tokyo, Los Angeles, Atlanta, Miami, Paris, New York, and more. This is a "don't miss" travel website.

FIGURE 2.12
Select the Travel menu choice at MSNBC for a plethora of travel information.

The Travel Channel is a popular cable television channel. You can get plenty of ideas from watching its travel shows, but you can also get a plethora of information from the Travel Channel website at http://travel.discovery.com. You will find vacation ideas, travel tools, travelers' reviews, podcasts, and, of course, TV show schedules. Like many other TV stations, the Travel Channel is experimenting with putting its television programming on the Web. It has everything from short clips to full-length travel programming available for your online viewing. Whether your destination is domestic or exotic, the Travel Channel is a good place for information.

Finding Your Way Around

This is where I must confess that one of my biggest shortcomings is that I am directionally impaired. Show me a new computer, and I can find my way around with ease, but put me in an unknown location, and I can't find the pizza parlor three blocks away. Perhaps that's why I have fallen in love with global positioning systems (GPSs) and Internet mapping websites.

Global Positioning Systems

Global positioning systems, often called GPSs, offer hope to all those who struggle to find their way around.

You can purchase a GPS in many different configurations. Car units are the most popular. These can be built into the dashboard as an option when you purchase the car or can be added later. Other popular units attach to the windshield with plastic feet. You can also purchase a GPS as a handheld unit that can help you get around when on foot.

The GPS uses satellites to pinpoint your current location. The software in the unit can contain maps of any area of the world. You simply put in the address of the location you want to travel to, and the GPS tells you how to get there. All have small screens that show you a map with the route. All give on-screen directions. GPSs that are made for cars also give you voice directions.

Because the GPS always knows exactly where you are, it can alert you to the next turn in advance by saying something like "Turn left in 300 feet."

Most GPSs also include information on restaurants, gas stations, ATMs, and other points of interest. So if you are on the road and looking for a place to eat, your GPS can find one for you.

LINGO

GPS stands for *global positioning system*. This is a navigation system formed by 24 satellites orbiting the earth that can read the exact location of a GPS receiver.

These systems are fantastic for taking road trips and can also be used to get you to the museum you are searching for in a foreign city.

Mapping Sites

The Internet is also a great resource for helping you get around. Free mapping websites pinpoint any location, giving you maps of locations around the world. At these sites you simply enter the location's address, and a map showing that location appears. Figure 2.13 shows a typical map from the MapQuest website.

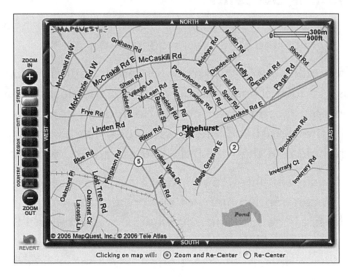

FIGURE 2.13
MapQuest and other mapping websites provide detailed area maps.

If you enter your starting location, you can also get step-by-step directions to that location. You even get the exact distance to be traveled and, in some cases, an estimated amount of travel time.

Many of these websites also help you locate restaurants, hotels, and other points of interest. Some even include traffic reports.

Here are four of the most popular mapping websites:

- Google Maps: http://maps.google.com
- MapQuest: www.mapquest.com

- MapsOnUs: www.mapsonus.com
- Yahoo! Maps: http://maps.yahoo.com

No Planning—Just Get Up and Go

I know you're out there. You just want to get up and go and don't want to bother with all that planning stuff. Well, the Internet has you covered. In fact, sometimes when you can just pick up and go, you can get some great deals. If this is your type of vacation, check out these websites:

- 11th Hour Vacations (www.11thhourvacations.com) is a great place for last-minute opportunities. Most travel bargains are announced about a month in advance, but you will also find listings for next week and a few for two months down the road.

  If you're always on the lookout for last-minute bargains, sign up for Louie's Savings Alert, e-letters that notify you of eleventh-hour travel deals at www.11thhourvacations.com.

- LastMinute Travel.com (www.lastminutetravel.com) has an expansive list of hotel openings, flights, and vacation packages with substantial discounts. Check out the Top 20 Deals for some real last-minute bargains. In addition to photos, this website also features videos and virtual tours of some of the offerings.

- Moment's Notice Travel (www.moments-notice.com) caters to procrastinators. It has bargain-basement prices on last-minute cruises, vacations, flights, hotels, and car rentals.

What to Pack

If you are anything like me, after you've decided where to go, you immediately wonder what you should pack. As usual, the Internet can help you pack just what you need.

Sandy's tip
Create a Trip Packing list of all the usual things you need on a trip, and use it every time you travel. You'll never forget your camera or sunglasses again!

First, you need to check the weather. On the Internet, that's easy. Just surf to www.weather.com, where you can enter almost any city and get a weather forecast. You can also get the weather forecast for the next month as well as useful weather averages for the time of year you will travel. Click the World tab if you will be traveling outside the U.S. The World Weather area gives you links to local weather websites, which can be even more accurate for your short-term planning.

You may also want to visit Weatherbase at www.weatherbase.com. This site has comprehensive information on 17,000 cities worldwide. You can check the average snowfall in November in Zurich or see how much rain usually falls in Seattle in February.

After you know what the weather is most likely to be, you can start planning your packing. The Frommer's Travel Planner (www.frommers. com/tips/packing_tips/travel_planner.pdf) is a printable pre-trip checklist that can help you plan your packing.

You may also want to use the Universal Packing List website (http://upl.codeq.info), shown in Figure 2.14. It lets you customize a packing list geared to the temperature and your activities. It may be just what you need to jog your memory about taking your contact lenses or beach hat. You can also use it as a place to start in creating your own customized packing list.

Sandy's tip
If you're tired of pulling heavy luggage and struggling with overstuffed bags, visit OneBag. com (www.onebag.com), where Doug Dyment shares his expertise on traveling light.

Another place to look for packing advice is the FabulousTravel.com website tips area at www.fabuloustravel.com/tips/tips.html. I especially like its lists of "12 Things to Pack That Might Not Occur to You" and "Tips for Traveling with Carry-On Luggage."

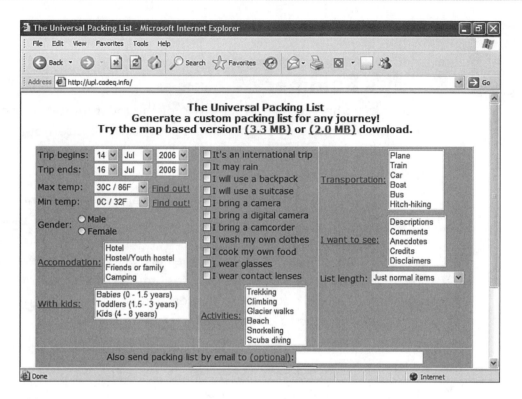

FIGURE 2.14
The Universal Packing List guarantees that you have everything you need for your trip.

Last but not least, if you are a fan of television travel star Rick Steves, you will want to check out his "Rick's Packing List" at http://ricksteves. com/plan/tips/packlist.htm. He gives a printable list with check boxes that you can use to cross off items as you gather them or as you pack.

Sandy's Summary

Where to go and what to do are two of the most important decisions you will make when planning a getaway. The Internet is an extraordinary travel resource for finding destinations and planning a trip.

Travel websites are filled with information and ideas that help you plan your trip. Old travel favorites such as Frommer's and Fodor's now have a Web presence with plenty of travel information. Many newspapers and magazines are also online now and offer travel articles, destination guides, and a plethora of other travel information. Local tourism sites give you the scoop on what their area has to offer.

There are even websites that let you know what the weather will be like and how to pack.

The best part is that all this information is free.

Internet resources will have you on your way to your best trip ever in no time at all!

Sandy Berger

Chapter 3

Bargains Galore

I have found out that there ain't no surer way to find out whether you like people or hate them than to travel with them.

—Mark Twain

Computers and the Internet have revolutionized the travel industry. Just a few years ago, booking airline tickets, cruises, and hotel rooms was done by travel agents who charged a fee for their services. Today, the average traveler can compare prices online and book his or her own tickets without additional fees. In fact, online resources often help you find bargain prices.

These changes have also opened the leisure travel industry to a larger segment of the population. Years ago only the upper class could afford leisure travel, but today travel has become an everyday part of life for the average person, who looks forward to vacations and personal travel.

In This Chapter

- Online Travel Services
- Travel Search Engines
- Real Bargain Hunting
- Naming Your Own Price on Priceline.com
- Deal Alerts
- Discounts on Hotels
- Travel Scams

Changes in the travel industry have not been lost on baby boomers and older travelers. With more time on our hands, seeing the world has become a goal for many boomers, and Internet resources help us do it affordably.

Online Travel Services

Online travel services have become one of the main places to look for travel bargains. Many of these travel websites negotiate rates with air, car, and hotel companies. Many of these websites are very popular and can offer rates that cannot be matched anywhere else.

BLOOPER ALERT
Be aware that Expedia, Travelocity, and Orbitz all have booking fees that range from $5 to $16.

The three largest online travel service sites are Expedia, Orbitz, and Travelocity. Websites such as these focus on selling you tickets, and in order to do so they must have appealing prices. Each of these websites helps you compare prices and make reservations for hotels, flights, rental cars, and cruises. They also allow you to book package deals for as many of these services as you need.

Travelocity.com

Travelocity (www.travelocity.com) is one of my favorites because it allows you to search for exact dates or flexible dates easily, as shown in Figure 3.1. When you must be in a certain city on a certain date, you can use the exact date feature. When it doesn't matter whether you are there on the 4th or the 6th, you can use the flexible date option. Using flexible dates often allows you to get better fares because many airlines offer lower rates if you fly on specific days at specific times. Another nice feature in Travelocity is that if you click "Compare surrounding airports" you can sometimes find alternate airports that have cheaper fares.

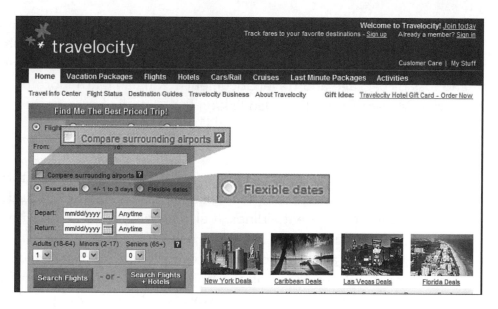

FIGURE 3.1
At Travelocity you can easily search for flexible dates and consider travel to alternate airports that may help save you money.

Expedia.com

Like Travelocity, Expedia (www.expedia.com) helps you find and book flights, hotels, cars, cruises, activities, and packages. It also has options for searching for flexible dates and one-way trips.

Expedia is also the leader in an area called Dynamic Packaging. This allows customers to package hotels, cars, and flights in any manner they choose rather than being forced to use the prearranged packages offered by airlines and hotel vendors.

Expedia has a taken a step in the right direction in helping consumers by initiating a best-price guarantee. Unfortunately, it is pretty restrictive. You must find a better price online for the exact same trip, and you must notify Expedia within 24 hours of your booking to get a refund of the difference between the two fares and a $50 travel coupon.

Expedia also has a Package Protection Plan that covers you if you cancel your trip for any reason. This $39-per-traveler insurance plan also covers certain travel and baggage delays, travel accident protection, and loss of baggage and travel documents. You can learn more by clicking the Package Protection Plan link on the Expedia home page.

Orbitz.com

Orbitz (www.orbitz.com, shown in Figure 3.2), the last of the big three online travel sites, is excellent for finding airfares because it includes airfares from 450 different airlines. It also allows you to choose flexible dates, but this feature is not as easy to use in Orbitz as it is in Travelocity. Orbitz also lets you find fares for multicity trips, which some other travel sites don't offer. Orbitz makes it easy to order a special meal and to choose your seat in advance. It also shows you the total duration of a multileg journey, which most other travel sites don't.

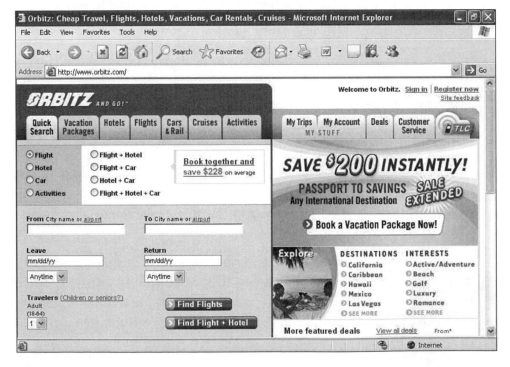

FIGURE 3.2
Orbitz helps you find the best price on flights, hotels, cruises, cars, and vacation packages.

Other Discount Sites

Although you can find great deals on sites like Travelocity and Orbitz, they don't list fares for certain airlines, such as Southwest Airlines. JetBlue, AirTran, and Frontier are other discount airlines that are not always included on the major travel sites. So if you are looking for the best price and one of these discount airlines serves your city and your destination, be sure to check out its website directly.

- AirTran: www.airtran.com
- Frontier: www.frontierairlines.com
- JetBlue: www.jetblue.com
- Southwest: www.southwest.com

You will find many other online travel resources that use Expedia, Orbitz, or Travelocity as their underlying travel search engine. For instance, the NYTimes.com travel area uses Expedia's database. So you get the same results at NYTimes.com that you find at Expedia. AARP's Passport Travel uses Travelocity. For the most part it is better to use the travel websites themselves rather than going through some third-party setup, which is usually not as comprehensive as the original site.

Trivia

Southwest Airlines was one of the first to allow customers to make online reservations on its website. Now the majority of Southwest tickets are sold online, saving the airline millions of dollars in annual operating costs.

Sandy's tip

Special fares from these low-cost airlines are much less restrictive than the high-cost carriers' weekend specials.

Tips for Finding Great Fares on Orbitz, Expedia, and Travelocity

Each of the three major travel sites that we just talked about (Expedia, Orbitz, and Travelocity) have different listings and give you different

Sandy's tip

Each travel search engine and travel service has its own search logic and algorithm. Even though they include the same airlines and hotels, their search results may be different, so be sure to check out more than one.

Trivia

Expedia was founded as a division of Microsoft in 1996. It was later spun off and subsequently sold.

results when you search for the best prices. Each also has a different interface with a distinct way in which you input your information and get your results.

When I compared results on Expedia, Orbitz, and Travelocity, each one was the low-price winner for at least one of the pretend trips I entered. So you may want to look at all of them. See which one you find the easiest to use and which one seems to return the best prices for you. If you get familiar with all of them, you can perform your travel searches quickly and make sure that you are finding the best price.

If you need help on Travelocity or Expedia, both have 24-hour help lines. They help you navigate the site and find what you need. They can even book the tickets for you, although there may be an additional charge for that service. At the time I write this, Orbitz has only a customer service telephone line, and it is questionable whether they will actually help you navigate the website.

Expedia, Travelocity, and Orbitz have a fierce competition going. Right now most of their bookings come from airline sales, but they are all strengthening their offerings in cars, cruises, hotels, and packages. Expect to see even more innovations in the future as these travel services vie for your clicks.

These big three travel sites have also ventured into the business travel area, which traditionally has been the realm of traditional travel agents. The business travel websites are very similar to the leisure travel websites, with the addition of client profiles that have information such as a company's list of preferred hotel vendors, airlines, and rental cars. They are called Orbitz for Business, Travelocity Business, and Expedia Corporate Travel.

Travel Search Engines

Just about anyone who spends any amount of time on the Internet is familiar with Google, the most popular search engine in the world. Google has become all the rage because it provides a valuable service: it helps people find things on the Internet.

In like manner, many travel search engines have sprung up to help people find travel fares, hotels, and accommodations. The focus of these search engines, however, is not just finding you websites from which to purchase. These search engines are geared toward finding you the best prices.

Almost all of these travel search engines are free. They draw their data from a wide range of sources, but they don't actually process the bookings. Instead, like an Internet search engine, they list the results and give you a link to the Web offerings, which you can click to go to the website where you can make the purchase. These sites earn money from commissions on transactions and from advertising.

BLOOPER ALERT
The word "from" in travel offers means the starting price of the package or service. This often represents the smallest room and "off-season" pricing. The price you pay usually is much higher.

One of the benefits of using a travel search engine of this type is that you book your travel with companies and brands that you may have more confidence in than online travel websites. For instance, you go to the search engine and it presents you with the best price from American Airlines or Holiday Inn. Then you purchase your ticket online directly from American Airlines or Holiday Inn.

SideStep.com

SideStep (www.sidestep.com) is one of the oldest travel search engines. Over the years it has refined its interface and added useful features. SideStep is a popular travelers' search engine that looks for flights, hotels, cars, vacation packages, and recreational activities. SideStep searches multiple travel sites and presents you with the results quickly and easily. It searches more than 150 travel sites such as online agencies, consolidators, airlines, hotels, vacation package providers, and car rental companies. SideStep even searches Orbitz for you. It also includes JetBlue, Airtran, Holiday Inn, and Frontier Airlines. Southwest Airlines is not included, so you still have to search there separately, but because so many websites are included, SideStep can considerably cut down the number of websites you need to search.

SideStep also has a free toolbar that you can use with your Web browser. This toolbar is available only for the Internet Explorer Web browser, but if you use Internet Explorer, you may find it beneficial. It installs easily and appears as an airplane icon on your browser's toolbar, as shown in Figure 3.3. Just click the airplane when you are looking for a travel bargain. You see SideStep's choices alongside the results from Expedia, Travelocity, and other major websites, making comparison travel shopping a little easier.

Kayak.com

Kayak (www.kayak.com) is a travel search engine that is known for finding inexpensive flights, as well as hotel deals, car rentals, and vacation package deals. It searches for flights from more than 120 websites. Kayak also offers fare alerts by email and forums where users share tips and ideas. Kayak lets you search flexible dates and preferred airlines.

As shown in Figure 3.4, the Kayak website has a very simple, uncluttered interface that lets you work with the search results quite easily. You can use slider bars to adjust the departure and arrival times, and you can easily check or uncheck the airlines and airports.

FIGURE 3.3
You can start the SideStep toolbar by clicking the airplane icon on Internet Explorer's toolbar.

Kayak has several very useful features. It remembers your searches and lets you access them from anywhere, and it automatically lists the 25 destinations that were most searched for on Kayak for the past two days from the airport of your choice. This list is presented in a graphical manner using Google Maps. You may find this an interesting way to find a destination when you have nothing in mind except the thrill of seeing some new sights.

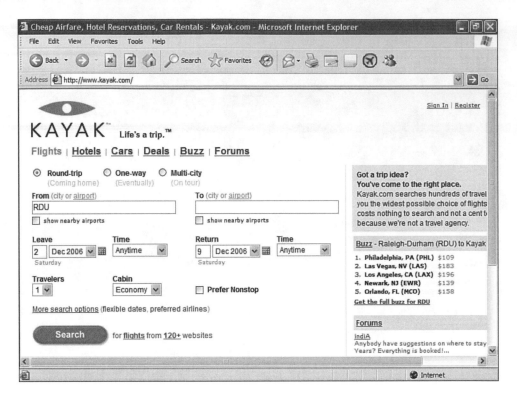

FIGURE 3.4
The Kayak website is simple but powerful for finding travel bargains.

Yahoo! FareChase

Another good free travel search engine is Yahoo! FareChase, which can be found at www.farechase.yahoo.com. FareChase focuses on flights and hotels. The interface is similar to most of the other travel search engines where you enter your starting point, destination, and departure and return dates. FareChase lets you search for better deals from nearby airports, search for either round-trip or one-way fares, and add stops you may want to make on the way.

FareChase is also experimenting with new tools and features. It has two widgets that you can download, as shown in Figure 3.5. These small pieces of software reside on your desktop so that you can see them anytime without clicking over to the FareChase website. Click the Yahoo! FareChase Tools link on the FareChase home page to get more information about the widgets.

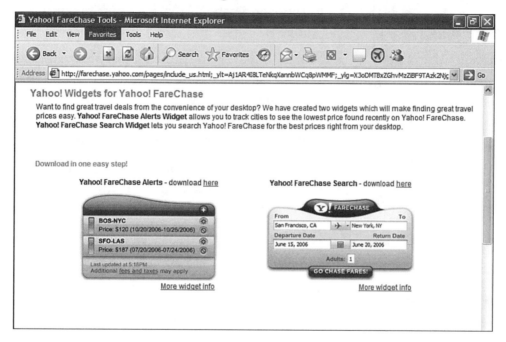

FIGURE 3.5
Yahoo! FareChase provides free widgets that you can download to your desktop for easier travel searching.

The first widget is called FareChase Alerts. It lets you know when a special fare you may be interested in becomes available. The second one is FareChase Search, which lets you search for FareChase fares without having to visit the FareChase website.

Mobissimo.com

Mobissimo at www.mobissimo.com is a search engine that has a large network of

LINGO

A *widget* is a small piece of software that adds functionality to a larger program. Widgets usually are small applications that appear in a browser or on the computer desktop, showing the user helpful information.

international suppliers for airfares, hotels, and cars. The engine searches more than 171 travel websites for you. Besides foreign websites, it also searches Orbitz, American Airlines, JetBlue, and other American carriers and suppliers.

BLOOPER ALERT

You may think that standard negotiated discounts like AAA and AARP are the cheapest. This is not necessarily true. In my unofficial tests, Kayak and SideStep often found rates cheaper than the AAA or AARP discounted rates.

One nice feature about Mobissimo is that it has a tutorial for new users. Just click the New to Mobissimo? link at the bottom of the home page, and you are taken through a brief tutorial that explains the website and how to use it.

Mobissimo's foreign connections are extensive, with airlines, hotels, and car rental agencies all nicely represented. Mobissimo also publishes a list of which travel sites it searches. You can find it at www.mobissimo.com/faq.php#suppliers.

Fares and Fees to Consider

Although the big three online travel service sites (Travelocity, Orbitz, and Expedia) all add a service charge to your travel booking, only a few travel search engines charge for their services. Qixo at www.qixo.com charges $20 for each fare booked. Best Fares at www.bestfares.com requires a $60 membership fee. If the fares they find are cheap enough, they may be worth the price, but I am inclined to go with some of the many free travel search engines.

I have mentioned just a few of my favorite travel search engines. When I entered the term "travel search engine" into Google, I got 812,000 results. So obviously there are many more such search engines for you to investigate.

Real Bargain Hunting

If you are flexible in your travel dates and you would like to travel but you don't know where to go, the Internet will come through with plenty of ideas.

Websites like the following are noted for good buys:

- Airfarewatchdog.com: www.airfarewatchdog.com
- Cheapflights.com: www.cheapflights.com
- LastMinuteTravel.com: www.lastminutetravel.com
- SmarterTravel.com: www.smartertravel.com
- TravelZoo: www.travelzoo.com

Sites like these find bargains and consolidate them at their websites. They do not act like booking agents, but instead send their visitors to the company that is making the offer. Many of these are places to find real bargains.

TravelZoo.com

TravelZoo (www.travelzoo.com) is one of the more popular of these sites. TravelZoo aggregates deals from more than 500 travel advertisers. These travel companies pay TravelZoo to distribute news about their latest offers. TravelZoo states that it researches and tests its recommended deals before publishing them.

You don't purchase travel packages directly from TravelZoo. Instead, as with travel search engines, TravelZoo sends you to the website of the service provider to make the purchase. TravelZoo also has a weekly email newsletter featuring its most exciting deals.

BLOOPER ALERT

Be careful of bargain sites. If you are not familiar with the company providing the travel package or service, you will want to investigate thoroughly before you buy.

Figure 3.6 shows the TravelZoo home page. As you can see, some of these bargain websites may not be as well organized as some of the other websites we've looked at so far.

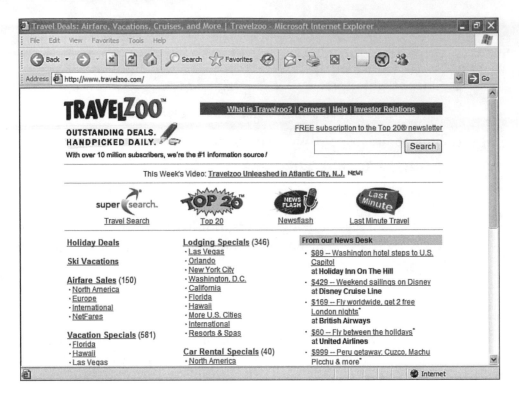

FIGURE 3.6
The TravelZoo website is a haven for bargains, but it is not terribly attractive.

Hotwire.com

Another bargain-hunter website is Hotwire (www.hotwire.com). Hotwire works with airlines to find unfilled airline seats and offer substantial discounts to fill them. These discounts are obviously not available until a few days before the fight. For you to use Hotwire successfully, your flight plans must be flexible. If you wait for a last-minute bargain from Hotwire and one doesn't show up, you may not be able to get an acceptable price on your ticket from other sources.

There is one other caveat when dealing with Hotwire. You choose the days you want to travel, but Hotwire picks the flight times, and you can't see them until after you purchase. The same applies to the number of connections. You don't see them until after you purchase. So be sure you have plenty of time and patience. The connections could be numerous.

Naming Your Own Price on Priceline.com

Want to get the very best price on your vacation? Try a travel bidding site, where you can name your own price.

Bidding websites are not for the faint-hearted or those short on time. It takes a time investment to do research, to learn the ins and outs of the website, and to be able to bid proficiently. However, bargains can be had if you have time and patience.

Just about everyone has heard of Priceline (www.priceline.com). It has been around since 1998 and is the granddaddy of travel-bidding websites. At Priceline and other travel-bidding sites, the buyer submits the price he or she is willing to pay for travel, and the website either accepts or rejects the bid. At Priceline you can bid on airline tickets, hotel rooms, vacation packages, cruises, tours and attractions, and rental cars. No one is bidding against you. You simply name your price, and Priceline lets you know if it is accepted.

If you have never used Priceline, you can get information about how the website and the bidding work by clicking the New to Priceline? Find out more. link on the home page, as shown in Figure 3.7.

Over the years, Priceline has tried its hand at selling cellular phones, groceries, and life insurance. Those other shopping services didn't pan out. However, Priceline is always trying something new. As I write this, Priceline is offering competitively bid home mortgages and loans through a third-party financial service.

Although Priceline dabbles in other commodities, the travel industry remains its main focus. It is fairly easy to use the website to make a bid. Deciding what to bid may be the most difficult part. To help you in that area, next to the Name Your Own Price box you see another box that you can click to go to an area where you can shop and compare prices to determine what you should bid. However, you will also want to do your own research on other websites to determine what the item you are bidding on is really worth.

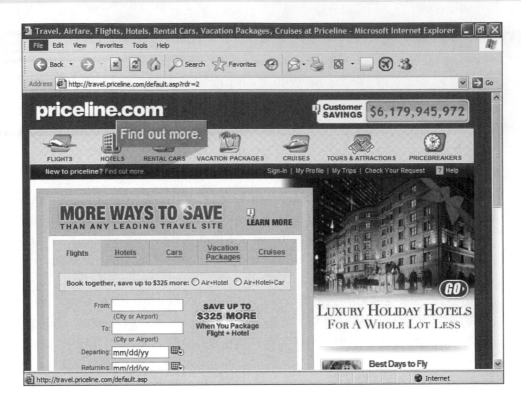

FIGURE 3.7
Priceline gives you an easy way to learn more about the website and how to bid.

Sandy's tip
Remember that visiting popular destinations off-season can save you money. Aspen and Zurmatt, two traditional ski resorts, are wonderful in the summer, even if you don't ski.

The one caveat on Priceline and other travel-bidding websites is that the bidding is blind. This means that you agree to pay for the item before you know exactly what you are getting. For instance, at Priceline, if you bid on a flight for certain dates and your bid is accepted, you must pay for the flight before you learn which airline you will be flying. Although you know the dates of the flights, you do not find out the exact times of the flights or the airline that you will be flying until you pay for the tickets. The same is true of hotel rooms. You do not know the exact hotel until after you pay for the room.

If you can live with these idiosyncrasies, Priceline may be right for you. If not, don't even try it.

Also, I have found some frustrations with the Priceline website. For instance, entering dates can be problematic. I entered 1-10-08, but my entry was rejected. I tried several other formats before I realized that the website wanted 1/10/08. You will no doubt find other frustrations, but it might be worth the trouble if you can get a cheap ticket or hotel room.

Most people use Priceline and other bidding websites by first searching the Web to find the lowest price available on the commodity they are interested in. Then they go to the bidding site and make an offer that is 10 to 20% lower than the best price they found. If they get it, great. If not, they usually have lost nothing. I say usually because a couple times, after being rejected by Priceline, I went back to the website where I found the best price, and the price was now higher.

Because Priceline is so popular, several websites actually focus on helping you make the most of your Priceline bids. One such site is Bidon Travel at www.bidontravel.com, where you can get tips on Priceline bidding for hotel rooms, cars, airfares, and vacations. As shown in Figure 3.8, Bidon Travel also has information on getting the best deals on Hotwire.

Priceline does not have its own message boards, but some other websites have message boards where Priceline users can ask questions and read about the experiences of others. Try the BiddingForTravel message board at www.biddingfortravel. com.

BLOOPER ALERT

Know the final price of the ticket before you buy. Read the fine print. Find out if service fees and taxes are included. Double-check whether the fare is one-way or round-trip. Don't get stuck with a trip you don't want or fees you weren't expecting!

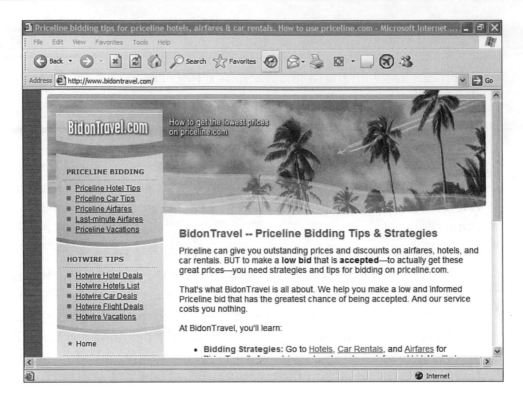

FIGURE 3.8
Bidon Travel gives you tips on using the Priceline and Hotwire websites to get the best prices.

Although Priceline is the largest travel-bidding website, many others are also available. Skyauction.com is one of them. From its name you might expect that Skyauction.com (www.skyauction.com) would offer only flights, but this is not the case. Skyauction.com, which is almost as old as Priceline, has a large variety of travel commodities. It features flights, hotels, cruises, vacation packages, and vacation rentals. It even has restaurant and entertainment passes. Skyauction.com is a true bidding site where you actually bid against others. Skyauction gives you a minimum bid. You register and add your own bid. You can also enter an auto-bid in which you choose the upper limit.

As you search the Web, you will find other travel-bidding websites. Be aware that each of them has its own bidding methodology and rules.

No matter which websites you use for your travel arrangements, you should always be careful. Read all the fine print so that you can uncover any hidden fees and understand any restrictions or limitations. Always investigate the cancellation policies. Each website has this information in different places, so you may have to do a little searching to find it, but the time you invest will be worthwhile.

Deal Alerts

What better way is there to get good prices than to have the offers come to you automatically? This may be easier than you think. Many travel sites will send you email alerts about their best deals. All you have to do is give them your email address, and the deals come rolling in. Here are a few of the major airlines that offer email alerts about great fares:

- American: www.aa.com
- Continental: www.continental.com
- Delta: www.delta.com (under SkyMiles)
- Northwest: www.nwa.com
- Southwest: www.southwest.com/email/emailSubscribe.html
- Spirit Airlines:www.spiritair.com (under the Special menu item)
- United: www.united.com
- US Airways: www.usairways.com (under the Specials menu item)

Check any airline that serves your departure city to see if it has email alerts that can save you money.

Many of the websites already mentioned in this book also have special email alerts that you may want to subscribe to. As you look through each website, keep an eye out for email alerts the site offers.

For instance, you will notice a FareWatcher email update that you can access from the Travelocity home page at www.travelocity.com. This

FareWatcher is a free personalized subscription service. You choose the pairs of cities that you might like to travel between. Then let the Travelocity FareWatcher send you email when changes to the airfare are posted for those cities. Figure 3.9 shows a sample FareWatcher email.

FIGURE 3.9
A Travelocity FareWatcher email can help you find the best air fares.

When looking for bargains, you will definitely want to also subscribe to the SmarterTravel email newsletter of special deals. You can subscribe to it at www.smartertravel.com.

Also, be sure to look for RSS feeds that can automatically collect information on special deals for you and deliver them to your desktop. The Orbitz Deal Detector at www.orbitz.com/dealdetector is one you don't want to miss. Just click the orange XML rectangle, shown in Figure 3.10, and follow the directions to get automatic offerings from the Deal Detector delivered to your Web browser.

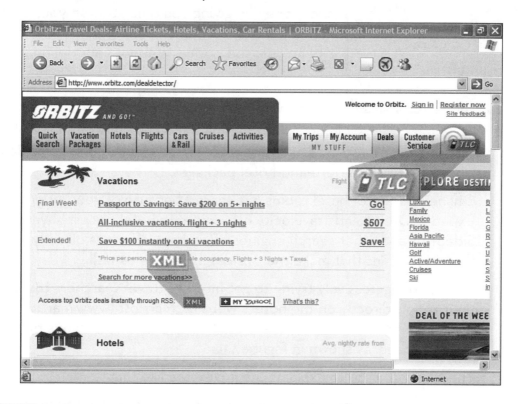

FIGURE 3.10
Click the orange XML rectangle to get automatic offerings from the Orbitz Deal Detector, or click TLC to get other special Orbitz offerings.

The Orbitz Deal Detector also has a link (shown in Figure 3.10) to an exciting new section called "TLC." This section has mobile alerts and information that can be sent directly to your Internet-enabled PDA or cell phone. These alerts give you information about your trip, including flight delays and cancellations, airport conditions and closures, gate change and baggage claim information, and bad weather and potential delays.

Sandy's tip
You can find more information on what RSS feeds are and how to use them in Chapter 1, "The Internet: An Amazing Travel Tool."

Even if you don't have an Internet-enabled handheld device, you can still use this area to get pre-trip email. These email alerts can save you time and money by giving you quick tips on your destination, including weather, confirmation, links to city guides, and podcasts about your destination.

Discounts on Hotels

Almost all of the online travel services and travel search engines also list rates for hotels. Often you can find good deals when purchasing airfare-and-hotel packages.

Online booking of hotel rooms has soared because of good pricing. Expedia, Orbitz, and Travelocity offer cut-rate hotel prices. Kayak, SideStep, and other search engines often have offerings directly from the hotel chains that make their prices attractive as well.

Hotels are aggressively trying to get Internet travel searchers to book their rooms directly on the hotel's website. Marriott (www.marriott.com) puts the information on its Best Rate Guarantee in an obvious place on its home page, as shown in Figure 3.11.

The Marriott website explains the guarantee like this:

> "Make a reservation with Marriott. Then, we'll give you the next 24 hours to look high and low for a better hotel rate. You can look anywhere. Look on the Internet. Call your travel agent or travel management company. Even double-check Marriott itself. If, in those 24 hours, you happen to find a lower rate for the same hotel, room type, and reservation dates, submit a claim form immediately. (You must submit the claim at least 24 hours before your hotel check-in time so we can properly verify each claim.) If the lower hotel rate you found qualifies, we will honor the lower rate and give you an additional 25% off that lower rate, subject to certain terms and conditions."

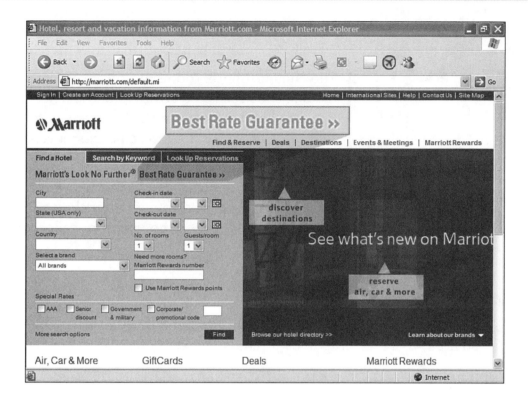

FIGURE 3.11
The Marriott Best Rate Guarantee is featured in a prominent place on the website.

Although 24 hours isn't a lot of time, it may be enough to make this guarantee worth the effort of searching for better rates.

Hyatt (www.hyatt.com) has a similar offer with an additional 20% off if you find a cheaper rate.

Basically what this means is that some of the large hotel chains are trying to lure people directly to their websites to make their reservations. And this is not necessarily a bad thing for the consumer. Often, hotel websites offer pictures and

Sandy's tip
Hotel telephones often have surcharges for long-distance numbers and charges for local calls. Use your cell phone and save money.

BLOOPER ALERT Some hotels deny award points to customers who book their rooms through third-party websites.

virtual tours of the hotel's rooms and amenities, so travelers can be sure about what they are getting.

The cheapest hotel rooms are often available on bidding sites such as Hotwire and Priceline. This is because hotel chains often deliberately undercut their own website prices to sell excess inventory.

When you read the fine print, all the hotel "best rate" guarantees exclude bidding sites where the hotel's name is not shown until after the nonrefundable room charge has been paid. Often the fine print calls these "opaque" travel sites.

Travel Scams

Always be careful when you are trying to get a bargain, because this is an area where unscrupulous businesses may try to scam you.

Sandy's tip Never pay with cash or a check. Using a credit card gives you better protection.

As you surf, remember that if an offer sounds too good to be true, it probably is. Be alert as you search for bargains. Websites often try to make the offer seem as cheap as possible. They might not be outright deceptive, but they may be good at massaging the truth and at advertising special rates that are almost impossible to get.

Some devious websites try to lure you by offering a price for a one-way trip and making you think it is a round-trip fare. When you are on an honest website, it will be obvious whether the fare is one-way or round-trip. Good websites spell out their service fees, surcharges, and taxes and let you know whether they are included.

Make sure that you are comfortable with the website you are dealing with. Also be sure that it lists telephone numbers and gives you a way to contact someone if you have questions or need information.

Although it might sound boring, be sure to read the fine print, especially on a website that you have never used. Before you hand over your credit card number, be sure you know the final price.

sandy's tip

If the rules for revisions, cancellations, and refunds are not clear to you, call the site's customer service number, and have them explain the rules and show you where they are on the website.

When surfing travel sites, you might come across travel scams that are designed to get your money. Discount travel clubs are popular ways to do this. Some respectable travel clubs charge a fee for membership. Just be sure that these fees are reasonable. Any club that asks for more than a few dollars is probably a scam.

If you are unfamiliar with the company you are purchasing from, always check it out. See if it is a member of reputable groups like the American Society of Travel Agents (http://astanet.com), the Association of Retail Travel Agents (www.artaonline.com), or the Cruise Lines International Association (www.cruising.org) .

Before you purchase, you can also check with the Better Business Bureau (www.bbb.org) to see whether the company has any complaints against it.

For tips about online safety and how to avoid travel scams, be sure to check out the American Society of Travel Agents' consumer site, TravelSense, at www.travelsense.org. As shown in Figure 3.12, this site has a Consumer Information section at www.travelsense.org/consumer/scams.asp that gives lots of good information on how to avoid travel scams.

sandy's tip

Don't expect personalized service from any website. If you want someone to take care of the details or hold your hand, use a travel agent.

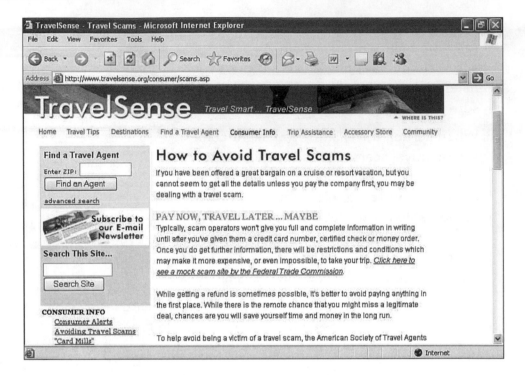

FIGURE 3.12
The TravelSense website has great information about how to avoid travel scams.

You will also want to check out the TravelSense website for travel alerts and additional travel tips.

Sandy's Summary

The Internet and online resources have redefined the travel industry. Years ago, a travel agent was the only one who could find and book travel for you. Wow, have times changed! The power to find great airfares and bargain-priced hotel rooms and vacation packages is now in the hands of the average computer user!

Online travel services like Expedia, Orbitz, and Travelocity make it easy to find good travel prices. They put it all together for you, and you can book directly through them.

Another type of online service has become very popular—the travel search engine. Websites such as Kayak, SideStep, and Mobissimo search many other websites, looking for travel bargains. Like Google and other Internet search engines, these websites give you a list of links where you can find great prices. These links take you to the websites that have the best prices on airfares, cruises, hotel rooms, and vacation packages. You can then purchase your tickets and make your reservations directly through the website that offers the best price.

Finding the best prices for travel can be fun, but you can also expect it to be time-consuming. As always, you must be careful in your choices. Remember that the more you learn about how to use your computer and the Internet to find travel bargains, the more successful and happy you will be!

Sandy Berger

Chapter 4

Tips for Air and Sea Travel

There are only two emotions in a plane: boredom and terror.

—Orson Welles

You already know that the Internet can help you find the best price for your plane or cruise ticket, but it offers other benefits for air and sea travelers as well. Luckily for us, the online travel industry is very competitive. This means that many websites offer additional resources to get our attention. Many of these offer conveniences for the traveler that make travel easier and more enjoyable.

Air Travel: The Price Is Right

There is a lot more to traveling by air than just getting on and off the plane. You also have to deal with getting boarding passes, navigating security, finding the right seat on the plane, and many other details. Don't worry, though. Your computer and online resources make it all easier than ever before.

BLOOPER ALERT

The old "stay over a Saturday night and save money" rule no longer applies. Midweek airfares are usually the cheapest.

Certainly you can use Travelocity, Expedia, Priceline, Kayak, and other travel search engines and services to get the best price on a flight, as discussed in Chapter 3, "Bargains Galore." However, there are even more places to look for great airfares.

For instance, the Cheapflights.com website at www.cheapflights.com helps you find the best deals from individual airlines. It also searches Travelocity, CheapTickets, Kayak, Orbitz, and many more.

Although most airline websites make you put in your travel dates, Cheapflights.com gives you a list of cheap fares and the dates they are available. This is very helpful for those who are flexible in their travel dates.

Cheapflights.com also has useful airline information at www.cheapflights.com/airlines. Twenty-nine airlines are listed. Figure 4.1 shows the guide for JetBlue (www.cheapflights.com/airlines/jetblue.html). This guide gives you much useful information about the airline. History, check-in times, baggage information, child fares, and other details are covered in depth.

Sandy's tip

Round-trip fares usually cost less than one-ways trips. So check them out and throw away the return ticket. You'll still save money.

If you need to search for specific dates, you can try a search engine like SideStep at www.sidestep.com/air. Like Cheapflights.com, this site allows you to search several airline websites, just by entering your information on the SideStep website. SideStep also searches airlines such as JetBlue, FrontierAirlines, and Airtran, which are not always included in other search engines.

Use a Nearby Airport

When you are booking an airline ticket, you will want to remain as flexible about airports as you can. Sometimes you can save a lot of money by using a neighboring airport. For example, it is often cheaper to fly to Newark, NJ instead of to a New York airport, and the distance to your destination in New York City may be similar.

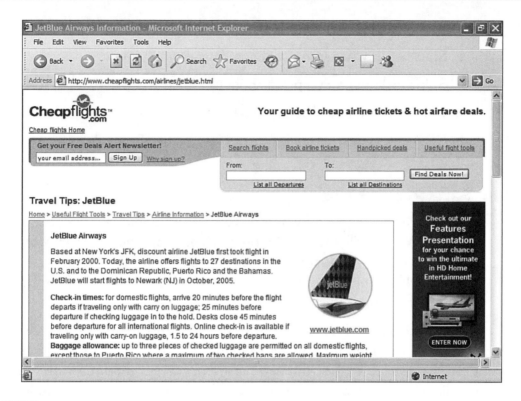

FIGURE 4.1

The Cheapflights.com website tells you everything you need to know about JetBlue and many other airlines.

Travelocity and Orbitz can automatically search nearby airports for you. Kayak and Cheapflights.com automatically perform that search and list neighboring airports in your search results.

Also, if you are flexible and you want a great fare, subscribe to the email from the various airlines. Each one offers weekly email that describes its specials for that week. Some are for travel during that week, but many extend into the future. Here are the links where you can sign up for this service:

- American: www.aa.com
- Continental: www.continental.com
- Delta: www.delta.com (under SkyMiles)

- Northwest: www.nwa.com

- Southwest: www.southwest.com/email/emailSubscribe.html

- Spirit Airlines: www.spiritair.com (under the Special menu item)

- United: www.united.com

- US Airways: www.usairways.com (under the Specials menu item)

Finding Fare Predictions

Have you ever wondered whether you should book that ticket or wait till later? When will you get the best price? Well, the Farecast website helps you determine just that. Farecast at www.farecast.com is an airfare search engine that also predicts how the price of an airline ticket will rise or fall over the coming days.

Farecast finds predictions for more than 75 cities. You simply pick your dates and destinations and click Go. As long as your dates and destinations are available (they appear in green), you get a notice with the fare predictions. For example, the route I chose in Figure 4.2 from Raleigh, NC, to Las Vegas, NV, told me to buy right now because the prices would be rising $50 or more within the next seven days. Farecast even gives a confidence rating. In this case it was 72% sure that the rates would rise.

Farecast also generates a list of scheduled flights and ranks them from cheapest to most expensive. The Farecast website is an interesting place to visit, even if you just put in a few pretend trips to see how accurate its predictions are. I did just that, and in my unofficial tests the site was correct more than 80% of the time.

Farecast is so sure of its predictions that it has a system called Fare Guard. Here's how it works. If Farecast tells you that the current ticket price is predicted to drop or stay steady, a Fare Guard button appears. Click the button to purchase a $10 Fare Guard to protect that lowest fare for the next seven days. In six or seven days, when you are ready to buy, if the lowest fare dropped since you purchased your Fare

Guard, you have paid $10, but you save money on the ticket purchase. If the lowest fare increased, you can use your Fare Guard to redeem the difference. It's quite a revolutionary idea! More details are available at http://labs.farecast.com/about/howFareGuard.jsp.

FIGURE 4.2
The Farecast website uses computers to generate predictions about whether airfares for a particular route will rise or fall.

While you are at the Farecast website, you might also want to check out its graph called Know When to Travel. You can access this from the Farecast home page. As shown in Figure 4.3, you see a chart of when the fares between the cities you chose will be the highest and when they are expected to be the lowest.

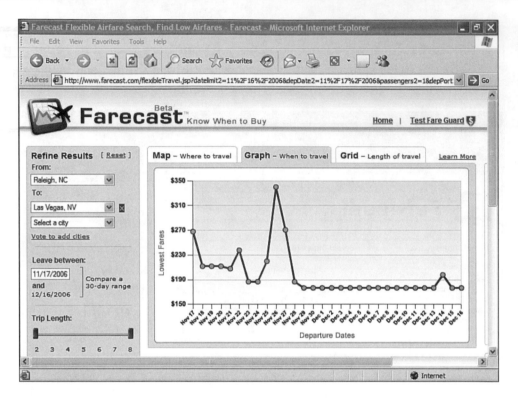

FIGURE 4.3
The Farecast website tells you when the fares between the chosen cities are expected to be the highest and the lowest.

Choosing an Airline

Although price is important, it is not the only criterion for choosing which airline to use. Your own experience is valuable in this area. If you would like a professional opinion on airlines and airports, surf to Skytrax at www.airlinequality.com. As shown in Figure 4.4, Skytrax provides airline star ratings and airport rankings. The airlines with the highest (five-star) ratings all happen to be outside the U.S—Cathay Pacific Airways, Malaysia Airlines, Qatar Airways, and Singapore Airlines. If you are a budget-minded domestic type of traveler, the four-star airlines include JetBlue, Frontier, and Virgin Blue.

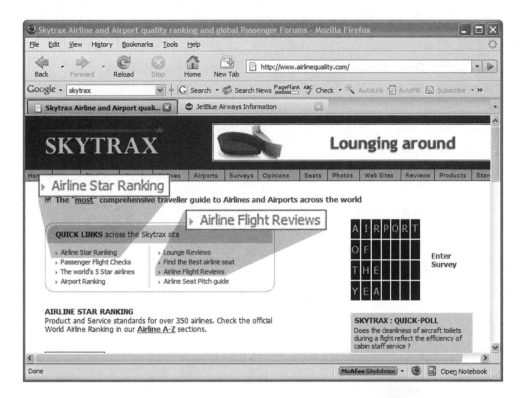

FIGURE 4.4
Skytrax rates airlines and airports.

Skytrax also has product and service standards for more than 350 airlines. The passenger opinions section contains forums for more than 480 airlines and 550 airports. The site also has peer reviews of airport lounges, flights, and airline seats. You can learn a lot about the various airlines and airports by reading the reviews of others.

For even more information about the various airlines, look at the Airline Quality Ratings (www.aqr.aero) by Dr. Brent Bowen and Dr. Dean Headley. This is a formal study and ranking of airlines that is published in several educational, travel, and research

Trivia

On May 1, 1981, American Airlines launched the first modern mileage program, unveiled as AAadvantage. It caused a marketing revolution that unleashed the many sophisticated loyalty programs available today.

journals. These ratings include on-time arrivals, denied boardings, mis-handled baggage, and customer complaints. As I write this, the Airline Quality Ratings rank the top ten U.S. airlines as follows:

1 Jet Blue

2 AirTran

3 Independence Air

4 Southwest

5 United

6 America West

7 Northwest

8 Continental

9 Alaska

10 American

These ratings are updated often, and the various criteria are listed by month, so visit the Airline Quality Ratings website for the most current ratings.

You can also visit AirlinesReviewed.com at www.airlinesreviewed.com for peer reviews of airlines. Perhaps you have a choice of airports, or you just want to be prepared by learning more about the airports you will visit. This website allows visitors to post their experiences with various airports and make them available for everyone to read Most reviewers list the top airports as McCarran International in Las Vegas, Baltimore Washington International, and Pittsburgh International. The two worst airports are usually John F. Kennedy in New York and Newark International in Newark, New Jersey.

BLOOPER ALERT

Airlines often command a premium price for nonstop travel. Connecting flights can save you money, but there is a cost—time and inconvenience.

Getting the Right Seat

The best seat on the plane is a matter of opinion. If you like comfort and a smoother ride, you may prefer a seat over the wing. If you are jittery about flying, a seat near the exit may be for you. For a quieter ride, you may want to sit near the back but away from the galley and restrooms. For added legroom you will want to find a first-row seat or sit in an exit row.

Every airplane has its own unique configuration. Depending on the plane's size and seat arrangement, Seat 9A may be near the front, or it might be the last seat on the plane.

So how do you know which seat to choose? Again, online resources come to the rescue, with several websites that can help you find the best possible seat.

LoveMySeat.com at www.LoveMySeat.com (shown in Figure 4.5) covers 50 airlines, including United, American, and Southwest. It lists more than 350 different planes. This comprehensive website has color-coded seating charts of each type of plane. It codes the seats as bad, below average, average, above average, partial recline, and no recline. It also gives ratings of each seat from visitors who have reviewed that seat.

Sandy's tip

If you have a flexible schedule, you may try to get bumped. When a flight is overbooked, the airline asks for volunteers to give up their seats and take the next flight. The compensation for this inconvenience is usually a free round-trip ticket within the U.S.

LoveMySeat.com also has excellent information on each airline, including website links, telephone numbers, hubs, frequent-flier programs, and other helpful information.

SeatGuru.com is very similar to LoveMySeat.com. It covers slightly fewer airlines and types of planes, with a list of 40 airlines and an airplane seat map of more than 275 planes. Yet it has great information about airplane seating. It also has color-coded seating charts. One of the SeatGuru features I like best is that when you hover the mouse pointer over each seat, you get detailed information about that seat, including the amount of legroom, whether the arm rest is movable, where the tray table is located, and other useful information.

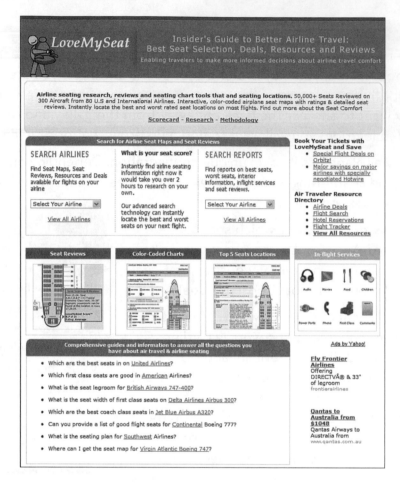

FIGURE 4.5

LoveMySeat.com offers seat reviews, color-coded charts, Top 5 seat locations, and in-flight services.

Sandy's tip

Choosing an emergency row can often give you extra legroom. These rows are for adults only.

In addition to airplane seating charts and information, SeatGuru also has comparison charts that give seat pitch, seat width, type of video, and the availability of laptop power for each airline and its type of aircraft. SeatGuru also provides in-depth information on how to identify your aircraft, explanations of bulkheads, and detailed articles on how to book the best airline seat.

Obtaining Boarding Passes and Using e-Tickets

With air travel, your use of the Internet begins before you leave home. If you saved some money by purchasing your tickets online, you can save some time and effort by printing your boarding pass before you leave home. Most airlines let you do this 24 hours before departure.

You use the paper document that you print exactly as you would a boarding pass that you get from the airline agent behind the desk at the airport. You show it for entrance to the security check area as well as for entrance to the plane. Printing your boarding pass at home has several advantages. The first is that you don't have to wait in line to have your ticket processed at the airport. This alone can save you a lot of time.

The second big advantage comes if you are flying an airline like Southwest that has no assigned seating. In cases like this, seating is often done by zones, with Zone 1 (or Zone A) being allowed to board first. If you check in at the airport, you are likely to be at the end of the line, with your boarding pass marked Zone 8 or 9. However, if you print your boarding pass at home 24 hours in advance, you are likely to be in Zone 1 or 2. This allows you to be one of the first to board the plane,

Trivia

A recent Gallup Poll showed that 60 percent of air travelers say they've experienced at least a minor problem with seat comfort. Nineteen percent said that airline seat discomfort was a major issue.

LINGO

In airline lingo, a nonstop flight means just that, but a *direct flight* means that there is an en route stop without a change of airplanes.

Sandy's tip

You often get only one chance to print your boarding pass, so be sure your printer has toner and paper and is ready to print when you start the process.

letting you choose the seat of your liking and assuring you that there will be room in the overhead bin for your roller bag or other belongings.

If you printed your boarding pass at home and you have only carry-on luggage, you can proceed right through security to your gate without standing in any ticket-counter lines. If you have luggage to check and you printed your boarding pass, you can check your bag curbside, or you can go inside and have an agent tag it. The lines for this are much shorter than those for obtaining a boarding pass.

If you booked your ticket online, but for some reason you couldn't print your boarding pass at home, you can wait in line at the ticket counter, or you can use one of the kiosks that every airline now provides.

An e-ticket holder can go to the ticket counter to check in, but it's faster to use a kiosk. Simply insert your credit card (for purposes of identification only), and the kiosk prints your boarding pass. Depending on the airline, you can immediately drop off your bags as well. You can't do this with a paper ticket.

Using Airline and Airport Websites

Whenever you travel by air, it is good to visit the website of the airlines you will be using before you leave. These websites have valuable information. This includes information on

- Current security rules
- Baggage restrictions, including size, weight, and excess charges

- In-flight services
- Special needs such as wheelchairs and special meals
- Airport check-in
- Airport lounges

Most airline websites also have airport maps and information on ground transportation. However, you will also want to check out the websites of airports that you will be passing through. Airport websites are more likely to have information on parking, concessions, and airport shopping than airfare search sites.

It is usually easy to find the website of the airline and airports you will be using. Just surf to Google (www.google.com) or any search engine and type in the name of the airline or airport. You will probably get a link to the airport or airline you are looking for.

For another easy way to find illusive websites, you can visit AirlineAndAirportLinks. com at www.airlineandairportlinks.com. This website lists airlines and airports by city, region, and airport code. It is a great place to find out what unusual airport codes stand for, as well as to get a link to some of the smaller airports that you can't find otherwise.

Sandy's tip

Many airports now have "cell phone parking lots" where people waiting for flights to arrive can park free of charge and wait for their passengers to call when they are ready to be picked up.

Trivia

The airport code ORD is used for O'Hare Airport in Chicago because when it was established in 1943, it was named Orchard Place/ Douglas Field. At that time it was one of the largest aircraft manufacturing facilities in the country. After World War II it was renamed Orchard Airport, and later the name was changed to O'Hare Airport after Butch O'Hare, a war hero and son of a Chicagoan who was murdered by the mob.

Booking Cruises

As with air travel, many websites can help you find just the right cruise. All the major travel search engines have cruise sections. These include the following:

- Best Fares.com: www.bestfares.com
- Booking Buddy: www.bookingbuddy.com
- Expedia: www.expedia.com
- Hotwire.com: www.hotwire.com
- Orbitz: www.orbitz.com
- Priceline.com: www.priceline.com
- Smarter Travel: www.smartertravel.com
- Travelocity: www.travelocity.com
- TravelZoo: www.travelzoo.com

In addition, many websites are dedicated to information about cruising.

The Cruise411.com website at www.cruise411.com is a good place to start your plans for a great cruise. As shown in Figure 4.6, you can search for a cruise by destination, cruise line, cruise length, and/or date. At Cruise411.com you can search for last-minute deals and book sailings on 20 different lines. This website is filled with valuable information on many different cruise lines including pictures of the ships and staterooms, and deck plans.

You can use many other online cruise agencies to compare prices. Cruise Value Center at www.cruisevaluecenter.com boasts that it is "America's Leading Cruise Broker." It has an extensive cruise finder, plus information on many different types of vacations. CruiseBrokers.com at www.cruisebrokers.com is a large retail cruise agency based in Tampa, Florida. Its online arm offers last-minute deals, luxury cruises, and special offers. CruisesOnly.com at www.cruisesonly.com is another online cruise agency that may be useful in getting cruise information.

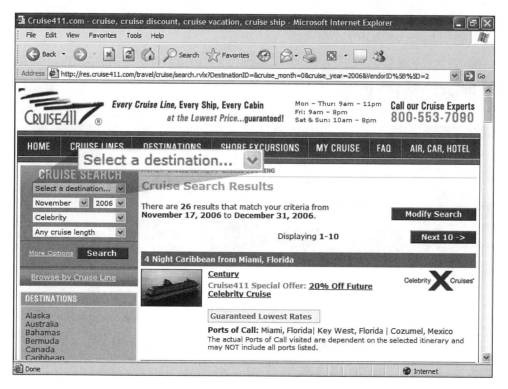

FIGURE 4.6
Cruise411.com lets you search for a cruise by destination, cruise line, length of cruise, and/or date.

Just as with air travel, you can always check out the travel search engines and online cruise agencies and then go directly to the cruise line website to compare prices and packages.

You will find that many of the cruise websites have special packages for "seniors." Often they are mentioned with the other offers, but some websites like SmarterTravel.com have special areas where you can choose from cruise deals just for seniors, as shown in Figure 4.7. You can find this area at www.smartertravel.com/senior-travel.

BLOOPER ALERT
Cruise lines advertise certain itineraries and ports of call, but they may be under no contractual obligation to keep to these schedules. Always read the fine print, and choose a cruise line carefully.

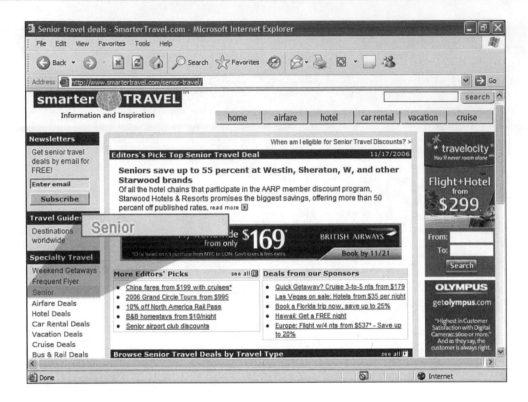

FIGURE 4.7
SmarterTravel.com has special cruise deals just for boomers and beyond.

If you want to get others' opinions of cruise lines, cruise ships, and cruise packages, check out CruiseOpinion.com at www.cruiseopinion.com. It has about 5,000 reviews that give opinions, ratings, and comments from other cruisers. It is a good resource for new cruisers as well as seasoned travelers who love the sea.

For cruise reviews, you will also want to check out CruiseMates.com at www.cruisemates.com. As shown in Figure 4.8, it features photo galleries, reader reviews, and message boards. This website also has information for first-time cruisers and single cruisers and other cruise information.

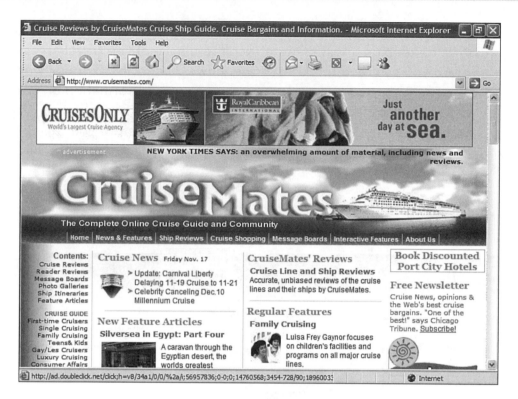

FIGURE 4.8
CruiseMates is an online cruise guide as well as a community of cruisers.

Many of the travel websites mentioned in this book also have information about cruises. For more excellent cruising travel tips, see Free Travel Tips at www.freetraveltips.com/Cruises. This site has information on how to get the best cruise price, how to pick a cruise, and how to choose a cabin. It's a great tip area for first-time cruisers.

There is no doubt that large cruise ships can be fun, but if you love the water, you may want to investigate cruising on a smaller ship. If so, you will want to check out the Small Ship Cruises website at www.smallshipcruises.com. It has information on how to charter a yacht and how to book a small-ship cruise. The site can arrange ships for weddings and anniversaries. It also has information on dive boats, river cruises, and much more.

The cruise industry is constantly changing. It is always good to read the news to keep up. Most major newspapers have online travel areas where you can read the latest travel news. The MSNBC Travel website at www.msnbc.msn.com/id/3032123 has specific information on cruising vacations plus message boards about cruises. Both are shown in Figure 4.9. You may want to check out the cruise news before you travel.

FIGURE 4.9
The MSNBC travel area has news about cruising vacations and cruise message boards.

Like other methods of travel, if you are flexible, booking cruises at the close of the cruise date may save you money. Look for last-minute deals in the cruise section of 11thHourVacations.com (www.11thhourvacations.com). Also be sure to check out LastMinuteTravel.com at www.lastminutetravel.com, which also has an extensive cruise area.

Sandy's Summary

Online resources offer many benefits to those who travel by air and by sea.

There are many places where you can search for the best price, so it is always good to develop a method of how and where you will search. This is especially important when you are dealing with airfares. You know that two people on the same flight may have paid two different fares, sometimes hundreds of dollars apart. You want to make sure that you are the traveler who paid the lower fare.

You also want to make sure that you choose the right airline. There are many places online where you can get reviews and ratings of airlines. While you are at it, you can use many different websites to learn about the airports you will be traveling through.

Online resources can also help you make your flight more comfortable. They can help you choose the right seat, eat at the best airport restaurant, and relax in the best airport lounge.

The same holds true with cruises. Online resources can help you choose the right cruise line and ship and also can help you get the best price.

So before you say bon voyage, be sure to use the many valuable Internet websites to make sure your trip will be the best ever!

Sandy Berger

Chapter 5

On the Road Again

We wander for distraction, but we travel for fulfillment.
—Hilaire Belloc

More than 80% of Americans take to the road for their vacation, and why not? It's a great way to see the country. Whether you travel by car, truck, RV, or motorcycle, technology has brought new travel amenities and travel helpers.

The Lure of the Road

If you grew up in the '50s or '60s, you understand the lure of the road. This was a time before superhighways...a time when the scenic Route 66 took you from Chicago to Los Angeles...a time when cars were plastered with travel stickers...a time when people jumped in their car for a Sunday afternoon drive.

In This Chapter

- The Lure of the Road
- Today's Blacktop Wanderers
- Hitting the Open Road
- Surviving at the Pump
- Navigation and Maps

Trivia

When Disneyland opened in 1955, an adult ticket cost $1.

The 1957 Jack Kerouac book *On the Road* was based on the spontaneous road trips of Kerouac and his friends as they traveled America's scenic roads. This book alone propelled many of us to hit the road. When we did, we listened to songs like "On the Road Again." It was first released by the Memphis Jug Band in 1928, and over the years the song has been repeated by artists such as The Grateful Dead, Bob Dylan, Canned Heat, and Willie Nelson. The song, like our fascination with road travel, literally spans decades.

Before we start our journey to websites that help you plan and execute your current and future excursions, why don't we let the Internet take us on a little trip down memory lane?

If you remember the old Nat "King" Cole song "(Get Your Kicks on) Route 66," you know that for many years Route 66 represented the romance and freedom of the automobile. For a look at this old scenic route, visit the Historic Route 66 website at www.historic66.com. Its slide show and turn-by-turn descriptions take you state by state. If you are up for a return to the old Route 66, this website leads you on your way, with step-by-step instructions for the journey. Click the Links area, shown in Figure 5.1, for a list of links to even more nostalgic information about Route 66.

Also, Route 66 fans will not want to miss the National Historic Route 66 Federation website at www.national66.com. This website is the work of a nonprofit organization dedicated to preserving Route 66. It gives the complete history of Route 66 and features a photo gallery of sites you may remember.

While you are in a nostalgic mood, be sure to visit the Driving Vacations through the Ages Web presentation for an interactive look at America's fascination with road travel. This MSNBC website is shown in Figure 5.2 and can be found at www.msnbc.com/modules/summer_driving/decades/frame.asp.

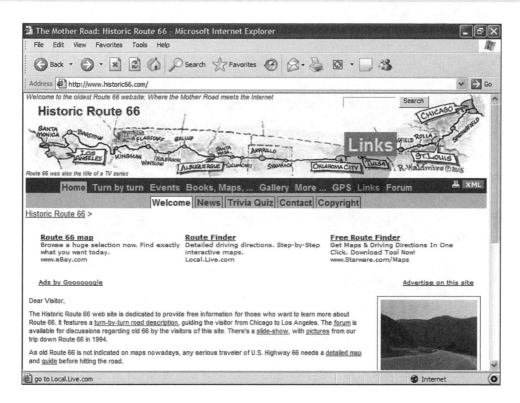

FIGURE 5.1
The many links in the Historic Route 66 website lead you on a nostalgic journey.

It presents a television-like presentation of how Americans have hit the road through the ages. Pick a decade, from the pre-1950s to the 1990s, and see the popular vehicles of the time, the cost of car trips, and popular destinations of that era. You can even listen to tales and see pictures of actual road vacations. You'll want to spend some time at this site. It is very well done and is sure to jog your memory. It has cars, roads, and plenty of memories. It even has an interactive calculator where you can see how much a road trip cost in the 1950s, when the average hotel room was $7 and the daily food bill for a family of four on the road averaged $6 a day.

Travel has changed quite a bit over the years. Superhighways let you get there faster, and the Internet helps you plan and execute your trip.

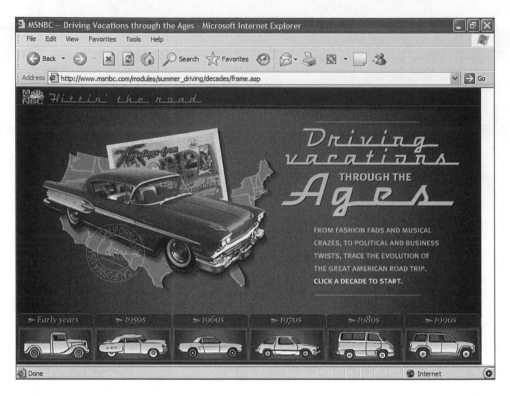

FIGURE 5.2
MSNBC Driving Vacations through the Ages takes you back in time to those road trips of yesterday.

Today's Blacktop Wanderers

After that "On the Road" fever hits, it is impossible to get it out of your blood. On top of that, road travel is often one of the most economical ways to go. Last July 4th weekend, the American Automobile Association (AAA) reported that more than 40 million people traveled, with 34 million of those holiday travelers going by car, in spite of the high cost of gasoline.

Today's blacktop wanderers include families taking vacations, dedicated RVers hitting the road, and motorcycle junkies who enjoy the wind in their faces. One of the biggest changes from the travel days of old is that most of today's travelers use online resources to help them get the most out of their trips.

Travel websites help you find things to do and places to go that you would not have otherwise known about.

Using the Internet to Find the Road Less Traveled

A great place to start your online journey is at America's Byways: National Scenic Byways Online at www.byways.org. As shown in Figure 5.3, you simply click the state you are interested in to find its scenic byways. This collection of distinct and diverse roads is sponsored by the Federal Highway Administration. The Byways Adventures page at www.byways.org/stories/1 is filled with road travel ideas that include romantic escapades, farming heritage, historic battlefields, presidential pathways, deserts, and highways of waterfalls.

FIGURE 5.3
The America's Byways website shows you the scenic way to go.

Many states also have a listing of their byways. For example, Colorado has a wonderful byways website at www.coloradobyways.org. Maine's byways website is at www.exploremaine.org/byways. You can find other states' byways websites by entering the state's name and the word "byway" into any search engine.

Often Internet resources can also help you find obscure roadside attractions and side trips that make the most of your time on the road. The America's Byways Pieces of Quirky Americana area includes George Washington's bathtub at Berkeley Springs, West Virginia, a 15-foot statue of Superman in Metropolis, Illinois, and a two-story outhouse in Gays, Illinois. The America's Biggest, Smallest, Hottest, and Everything in Between area features America's highest point, the largest freshwater lake in the world, the world's largest rubber stamp company, and much more. On the Historic National Road, which runs from Maryland to Illinois, you'll also find the world's largest bottle of catsup. It's 170 feet tall. This may be one of the only quirky sites that has its own preservation group, fan club, and official website. You can visit the website at www.catsupbottle.com, as shown in Figure 5.4.

For more offbeat tourist attractions, you may also want to visit Roadsideamerica.com at www.roadsideamerica.com. This site lists unusual tourist attractions and landmarks state by state. See the world's largest sundial in Arizona or ride a jackalope in Wyoming. There is something unusual here for everyone. Just think of the stories you can tell when you get home!

The Rand McNally site at www.randmcnally.com helps you with just about every aspect of your road trip. It has online maps, driving directions, and road trip planning. Its Explore America area at www.randmcnally.com/rmc/explore/exploreMain.jsp gives you an overview of every state in the Union, plus links to road construction and conditions. It also has rules of the road for each state. If you want to know unposted speed limits, the types of child restraints are required, or if studded tires are allowed, this is the place to visit.

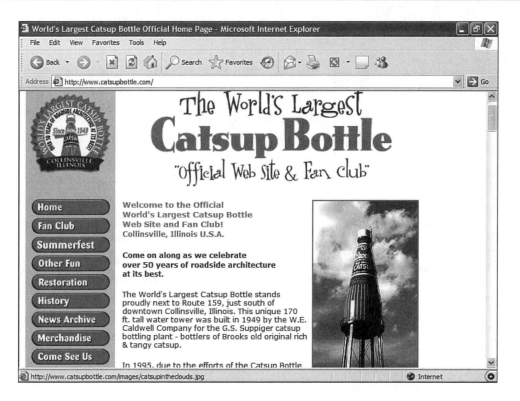

FIGURE 5.4
The Catsup Bottle website is home to the fan club of the world's largest catsup bottle, near Collinsville, Illinois.

TravelingUSA at www.travelingusa.com is a good online guide for road travel and recreation. Its Activities and Entertainment area has listings for everything from fishing holes to antique shopping areas. Its Travel Planning area includes listings for hundreds of Chambers of Commerce, visitors centers, and medical services. You can search each of these listings by type or by state.

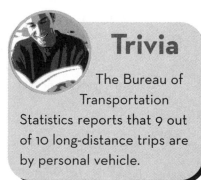

Trivia

The Bureau of Transportation Statistics reports that 9 out of 10 long-distance trips are by personal vehicle.

Sandy's tip

In case of an emergency on the road, be sure to have all the necessities, such as water, a blanket, jumper cables, and flares. Don't forget that a well-charged cell phone can be a life-saver.

RoadTripUSA at www.roadtripusa.com is the work of travel aficionado and author Jamie Jensen. You can read about his adventures or listen to his podcasts.

At one time the AAA was the authoritative guide for road travel in America. For decades dedicated road travelers went to their local AAA office before their trip for road maps and destination planning. Well, AAA is still an authority, but you no longer have to leave the house to get its information. You can do so right on your home computer. Just surf to www.aaa.com and put in your zip code to be transferred to your local AAA website. From there you can get information including maps and destination guides. Like at their local offices, some of the services require AAA membership.

Whether you are used to taking road trips or you are planning your first one, you'll find the Internet filled with useful road trip tips. For some commonsense advice, see FreeTravelTips.com. www.freetraveltips.com/RoadTrip includes tips on rainstorms, seatbelts, snacks, and how to avoid being the victim of a crime while traveling on the road.

Roadtrip at www.informationroadtrip.com is another useful site for the traveling man or woman. It contains traffic information, tips, and solid road trip advice to make your next excursion a little more stress-free.

WATCH YOUR SPEED—THEY ARE

One website to check out is the National Motorists Association (NMA) for information on motorists' rights. This member-supported organization promotes and protects drivers' rights on the road.

Much of the information on this website is free, but some is for members only. Check out the NMA's stance on the issues in the NMA Key Issues and Policy Positions section at www.motorists.org/issues. If you like the concept, you can join for $35 a year.

The NMA sponsors some very interesting Web services. Its Speed Trap Exchange at www.speedtrap.org lets you read about speed traps in North America that other Web visitors have posted. You can also add your own. www.speedtrap.org/ticket has information on how to fight a traffic ticket. Check out the informative area on Avoiding Future Tickets, shown in Figure 5.5.

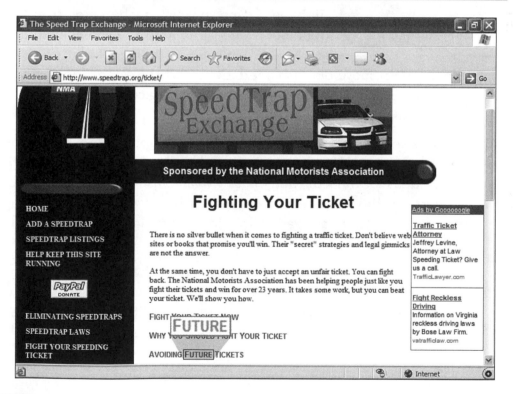

FIGURE 5.5
The Avoiding Future Tickets area of the Speed Trap Exchange website might just help keep you out of trouble on the road.

BLOOPER ALERT

The old common courtesy of flashing your lights at a car that does not have its lights on at night is now dangerous. Police report that some gangs drive around with their lights off and decide to victimize the first car that flashes its lights at them.

Traveling with Kids

Whether you are traveling with your children, grandchildren, or both, road trips with the family usually are pleasurable only if everyone is entertained and happy.

Why not use the Web and a few high-tech gadgets to keep everyone happy? Start with some old-fashioned road games. Remember when you used to form teams to count cows on rural stretches of road? How about 20 Questions? Or trying to spot license plates from all 50 states? Or the old Alphabet Game, in which each person tries to be the first to spot three items beginning with that letter before moving on to the next letter of the alphabet? For more old-fashioned ideas, visit the Roadtripplanning.com Road Trip Games area at www.roadtripplanning.com/road-trip-games.html.

The KidsHealth website at www.kidshealth.org/parent/positive/family/road_trip.html also lists Road Trip Boredom Busters. When you are looking for ideas for the kids, don't miss www.momsminivan.com. As shown in Figure 5.6, this website features 101 car travel games and road trip ideas for kids. There are games for kids, printable car games, travel games, and ideas for babies and toddlers.

When all else fails, consider turning to high-tech toys. Portable DVD players let the kids watch their favorite cartoons or movies. They keep kids entertained for hours on end. With the addition of headphones, the adults don't even have to hear the audio. The kids may not be looking at the scenery, but these video players are great for keeping the kids occupied during long stretches of boring highway.

Portable music players with ear buds are another way to keep the kids entertained. And don't forget portable game players such as the Nintendo DS and Sony's portable PlayStation. With the right games, these can be great for children of all ages.

FIGURE 5.6
The MomsMinivan.com website features travel games and road trip ideas for children of all ages.

Checking Out Road Conditions

Traveling on the road should be fun, so it's no picnic when you are caught in road construction or forced to take a detour. The Internet can help you plan your trip so that you can avoid such frustrations.

The most up-to-date information on the status of roads can be found on individual state websites. These websites give the location and status of construction projects, lane closures, weather-related problems, and other traffic information. The state websites can often be found at www.dot.state.*stateabbreviation*.us, where *stateabbreviation* stands for the two-letter state abbreviation. For example, the Wyoming Department of Transportation (DOT) website is at www.dot.state.wy.us,

Sandy's tip
For peace of mind, join a motor club that will help you out in case of a road emergency.

and the Colorado DOT website is at www.dot.state.co.us. Unfortunately, not all of the states follow this naming convention, but many do.

An easy way to get to a state's DOT website is to use the U.S. Highways Road and Travel Conditions website at www.usroadconditions.com. This site gives links to each state's highway road condition reporting websites. It is also filled with other interesting information, including links to live webcams from all states, traffic cams, weather, and ski conditions.

Hitting the Open Road

Now that the planning work is out of the way, it's time to decide what mode of transportation fits your fancy. Check out the following sections for tips and resources for traveling on two wheels, four wheels, or more!

Motorcycling

When you think of motorcycle riders, who do you think of? The black leather jackets and motorcycles of James Dean, Steve McQueen, Elvis Presley, and the Fonz have always epitomized "cool." Yet other motorcycle aficionados are not necessarily thought of in those terms. Did you know that Roy Rogers had a passion for motorcycles? As did George Bernard Shaw.

Yes, the love of motorcycling encompasses many different personalities. And it's not just for men anymore. Today more than one-third of the graduates of Harley-Davidson's Rider's Edge new-rider training program (www.ridersedge.com) are women.

In addition, many baby boomers who put away their motorcycles when the baby shoes appeared are now ready to hit the road again. Motorcycles are somehow equivalent to youth, and many boomers are ready to use them to ignite a youthful spark.

If you are a boomer who has always been interested in motorcycles, you may want to start your online motorcycle journey at the Motorcycle Hall of Fame Museum at www.motorcyclemuseum.org. The museum itself is in Columbus, Ohio, but the online version features current and past exhibits. The Classics area at www.motorcyclemuseum.org/classics/index.asp has some of the most interesting, groundbreaking, and weird motorcycles ever built, including the 1970 Harley-Davidson streamliner, shown in Figure 5.7.

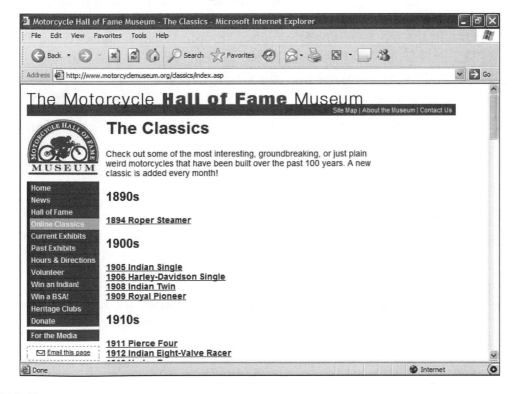

FIGURE 5.7
The historic 1970 Harley streamliner, shown in the online Motorcycle Hall of Fame Museum, was, for five years, the fastest motorcycle on Earth.

Motorcycle fans are a dedicated group, so there are several other motorcycle museums online. You can peruse them from your armchair or get on your bike and see them in person:

- Allen Vintage Motorcycle Museum: www.allenmotorsports.com

- Barber Museum: www.BarberMuseum.org

- The Rocky Mountain Motorcycle Museum: http://travelassist.com/mag/a20.html

- The Shop: American Motorcycle Museum: www.cycleshop.com/museum

- Wheels Through Time Museum: www.wheelsthroughtime.com

One of the most exciting things about motorcycling is participating in events. The Lets-Ride website at www.lets-ride.com is a great place to find rides, rallies, and biking events all over the world. Listing events is free, so if you know of an upcoming event, you can list it there to tell the world about it.

Check out the Links page on the Lets-Ride website at www.lets-ride.com/links for hundreds of links to motorcycling clubs and resources. As you scroll through the pages, you will be amazed at the number of links Lets-Ride has amassed.

The American Motorcyclist Association website at www.amadirectlink.com is filled with riding and racing information. As a protection and promotion agency, it also emphasizes rights resources and state laws.

More protection information can be found at the Motorcycle Riders Foundation at www.mrf.org. More motorcyclist rights organizations are listed at http://weaselsusa.org/mro.htm, where many state and international groups are listed.

As most cyclists know, state laws regarding motorcycle regulations vary greatly, especially helmet laws.

As of June 2006:

- Twenty states and the District of Columbia have a law requiring all motorcyclists to wear a helmet.

- Twenty-six states have a law requiring only some motorcyclists to wear a helmet.

- Four states do not have a helmet law.

So you may want to check the Internet to find out the current regulations of the states you will be visiting. The states do not have uniform Internet addresses for motorcycle information. For instance, Virginia's information is at www.dit.state.va.us. Minnesota's can be found at www.dps.state.mn.us/mmsc/latest, and Ohio's at www.motorcycle.ohio.gov.

You can use a search engine such as Google (www.google.com) to get information about each state by entering the state's name followed by the words "motorcycle" and "law." If you are just interested in the state helmet laws, check out the Insurance Institute for Highway Safety/Highway Loss Data Institute website at www.iihs.org/laws/state_laws/helmet_current.html. As shown in Figure 5.8, this website has up-to-date listings of the helmet laws in all 50 states.

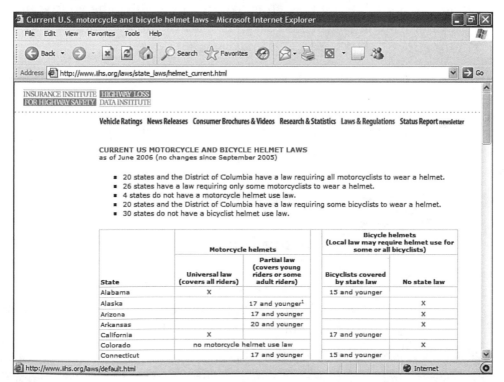

FIGURE 5.8
This website gives the helmet laws for all 50 states.

Car Care

When you are ready for that motor trip, you need to make sure that your vehicle is ready as well. If you are an auto expert, you know what to do. If, like me, you drive a car everyday, but you have little training in auto maintenance, the Internet is a wonderful tool.

Before a road trip, you need to prepare your vehicle for some nonstop wear and tear. Experts suggest that you check the tire pressure and rotation, inspect wiper blades, and check out the lights, fluid levels, belts, hoses, and battery. A good mechanic or knowledgeable neighbor can do this for you, but if you want to do it yourself, the Internet can help.

The Be Car Care Aware website at www.carcare.org was developed to help you learn how to take an active role in maintaining your vehicle. As shown in Figure 5.9, you can click any part of the automobile and learn more about how it works and how to maintain it.

Figure 5.9 also shows where to click to get to the Road Trip Preparation area of the Be Car Care Aware website. According to the website, each year neglected maintenance leads to more than 2,600 deaths, nearly 100,000 disabling injuries, and more than $2 billion in lost wages, medical expenses, and property damage. This site is dedicated to helping you maintain your vehicle. Its 10-minute pre-trip checkup could save your life.

LINGO

An **RV (recreational vehicle)** combines transportation and living quarters for travel and recreational purposes. These include towable travel trailers, motor homes, conversion vans, pickups, and SUVs.

Hit the Road in an RV

As soon as Henry Ford introduced his Model T, people started using cars for "auto camping." After World War II, the motor home industry flourished as Americans enjoyed the freedom of the road.

From the rounded silver Airstream trailers of the '40s and '50s to the classic Volkswagen "hippie" bus of the '60s, living on the road became a wonderful way to travel.

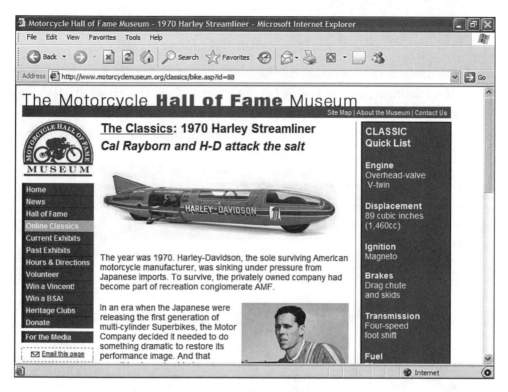

FIGURE 5.9

The Be Car Care Aware website helps you learn how to maintain your vehicle and how to prepare it for a road trip.

Today, RVs come in all shapes and sizes, including those with running water, air conditioning, DVD players, and all the amenities of home. Today's RV travel is more comfortable and convenient, yet it still offers travelers new surroundings, adventure, and appreciation of nature. It's no wonder that one of every 10 vehicle-owning households in the U. S. owns an RV.

It is also not surprising, then, that online resources for RVers are plentiful. RVTrips.com at www.rvtrips.com helps you plan your RV trip and acts as a wonderful travel guide. Just enter the origination of your trip, your destination, your route preferences, and the places you want to stop on the way, and RVTrips gives you a potential route. Unlike most mapping websites, this site gives campgrounds, RV dealers, travel plazas, and national parks as potential places to stop.

FunRoads.com (www.funroads.com), shown in Figure 5.10, is a great place for information about taking your RV on the road. Its RV Travel area has an Experience America section with RV travel and lifestyle articles, as well as sections on calculating directions, weather forecasts, RV safety, and cooking on the go.

FIGURE 5.10
FunRoads.com is a comprehensive website for RV information.

The Community area features forums, events, photos, and a newsletter. RVers like to stick together, so the FunRoad.com community area also includes a comprehensive listing of links to the websites of RV clubs (www.funroads.com/club/viewClub.jhtml). Some of the RV clubs are focused on a type of motor home or trailer. There is an Airstream club for vintage owners, an Alpenlite club, a Fleetwood American club, a Winnebago club, a Gulf Stream club, and many, many more. There are also many travel clubs, camping clubs, and discount clubs.

You can get a lot of information from RV owners' clubs. If you don't find your RV manufacturer listed at FunRoads, surf to the RVNetLinx website at www.rvnetlinx.com. Its list of RV owners' clubs and associations (www.rvnetlinx.com/wpclubs.php) covers about eighty different brands.

RVNetLinx also has a list of RV recreational clubs at www.rvnetlinx. com/wpclubs.php?cat=other. These clubs include clubs from certain areas, RV women's groups, military groups, camping clubs, and many more.

While you are at the RVNetLinx website, don't miss the other lists of Web resources provided on the home page. It lists campgrounds, parks, products, rentals, newsgroups, events, and manufacturers, to name just a few. Also, be sure to look at the top of the page, as shown in Figure 5.11, for a link to an interesting webcast television series called *RV USA TV*. This is a video series about RVing that you can watch on your computer at any time. You can travel along with the TV crew as they travel the Smokey Mountains, Pigeon Forge, Key West, South Florida, and more. I watched the two Missouri/Kansas programs, which focused on Route 66. Not only did I enjoy the programs, but I got information on RV parks to stay in while visiting the area.

Another website for RVers is RVtravel.com at www.rvtravel.com, which is filled with articles on destinations, camping, and online resources. It also has two unique sections on RVers Health and Historic Highways.

If you are interested in purchasing an RV, you won't want to miss GoRVing at www.gorving.com/pubs/rv_virtual_tours.cfm, where you can get definitions, descriptions, price ranges, and buying guides for all the different types of RVs.

BLOOPER ALERT

Driving or towing an overloaded rig is a leading cause of RV accidents.

LINGO

A *plug-in* is a small program that gives your Internet browser additional capabilities. It usually is free and can be easily downloaded to your computer.

This is also a good website to begin your search for a rental RV. It even has virtual tours of the different types of RVs at www.gorving.com/AM/Template.cfm?Section=RV_Virtual_Tours. These virtual tours allow you to see the entire RV in 360-degree surround views. The free IPIX plug-in that allows you do this is harmless and easy to install. You will find a link to download the plug-in at the bottom of the GoRVing virtual tour page.

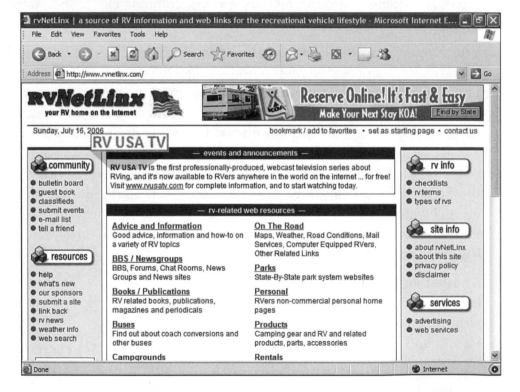

FIGURE 5.11
You can watch the *RV USA TV* videos on your computer at any time.

While you are at the GoRVing website, be sure to look around for the tips on driving and towing RVs and the Places to Go and Things to Do section in the Hit the Road! area.

The FirstRV.com website at www.firstrv.com also caters to first-time RV buyers. It lists RV vocabulary, reviews, sales, rentals, and campgrounds.

Interesting articles and information for RVers are available at many different websites. In fact, they are too numerous to mention here, but this list gives you an idea of what is available:

Trivia

Baby boomers account for the largest segment of RV ownership. They are also the fastest-growing segment of that market.

- RV Basics (http://rvbasics.com) has basic information, news, how-tos, RV maintenance, and repair.

- Your RV Lifestyle (www.your-rv-lifestyle.com) has advice for full-time RVers, including an RV lifestyle blog, RVer jobs, work on the road, and more.

- RVing Women (www.rvingwomen.org) offers support, information, and networking for women RVers.

- Find a RV Park (http://findarvpark.com/) helps you find an RV park. It includes a photo gallery.

- RV Camping (www.rv-camping.org) contains RV camping information on public lands, including checklists, camping, clubs, and RV news.

- RV Park Hunter (www.rvparkhunter.com) lists parks and campgrounds in the U.S. and Canada.

- Vintage Vacation homes (www.vintage-vacations.com) has a restoration shop for all types of vintage and classic travel trailers.

There is something for everyone when it comes to RV information. If you don't believe me, visit Bob Sokol's website at www.bobsokol.com/bus.html, where he shows how he converted a school bus into a motor home.

Visit any of the websites mentioned in this chapter and look for links to other websites and information. You are sure to find just what you are looking for, with little effort.

Surviving at the Pump

Trivia

In 1955, the average price of a gallon of gas was 23 cents.

Remember when you pulled into a service station and simply said "Fill 'er up" to have the attendant pump the gas and wash the windshield? I really enjoyed those good old days. With today's self-service gas pumps, I have to do all the work myself. On top of that, as we all know, gasoline prices have surged.

As Americans who love our freedom, high gasoline prices will not keep us from enjoying the open road. Some of us are taking shorter road trips. Some are taking them less frequently. All of us are thinking about ways to conserve gasoline. That's where the Internet can come in handy. Online tips for saving gas are plentiful.

Sandy's tip

The Environmental Protection Agency says average gas mileage decreases rapidly when you go faster than 60 miles per hour. For every 5 miles per hour you drive over 60, it's like paying an additional 15 cents a gallon.

According to the Environmental Protection Agency, you can save almost $700 annually by simply maintaining proper tire inflation and regularly changing your oil and air filters. Many websites remind us that good car care means better mileage and give maintenance tips. The Be Car Care Aware website has fuel-saving tips at www.carcare.org/road_trip.shtml. Its list of conditions that cause unnecessary use of fuel includes the following:

- Underinflated tires
- Dirty air filter
- Worn spark plugs

- Worn O2 sensor

- Dirty engine oil

- Loose gas cap

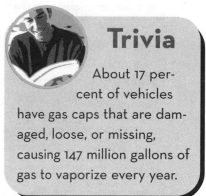

Trivia

About 17 percent of vehicles have gas caps that are damaged, loose, or missing, causing 147 million gallons of gas to vaporize every year.

The effects of each of these are given, along with the amount of extra gas they use.

As shown in Figure 5.12, the U.S. Department of Energy has an entire website dedicated to fuel economy at www.fueleconomy.gov. There is information on gasoline prices, hybrid vehicles, and alternative fuels, as well as mileage tips. More information can be found at the department's FreedomCAR & Vehicle Technologies Program website at www1.eere.energy.gov/vehiclesandfuels. This program is developing more energy-efficient and environmentally friendly highway transportation technologies so that we can use less gasoline.

Many states also have gasoline conservation tips. The New Hampshire Office of Energy and Planning provides an especially comprehensive list of tips at www.nh.gov/oep/programs/energy/conservation_gas.htm. These tips include how to drive to lessen gas consumption and how to purchase a fuel-efficient vehicle.

Don't overlook the consumer resources that many oil companies provide. For example, Shell Oil's website at http://localshell.com has fuel-stretching tips and fun facts about fuel. The Shell website even explains things such as octane ratings.

Looking for the best gasoline prices in your town, or the area you are traveling in? You can drive around and check out all the local stations, but then you would be wasting gas to find the cheapest price. So, why not use the Internet to find exactly what you need?

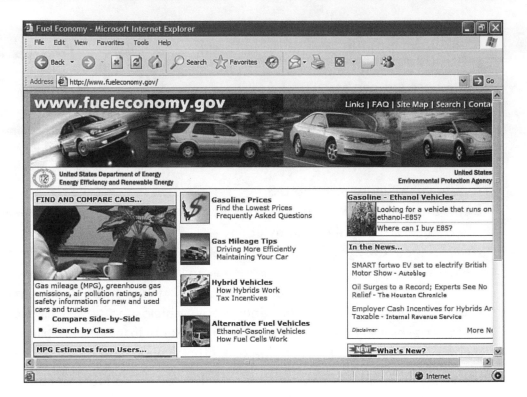

FIGURE 5.12
The Fuel Economy website is dedicated to helping people use their vehicles more efficiently.

You can go several places on the Web to get local gas prices. The most popular is probably GasBuddy.com at www.gasbuddy.com, shown in Figure 5.13. This site is operated by GasBuddy Organization, Inc., a non-profit organization. GasBuddy is a portal site for more than 170 similar websites that compare local prices. GasBuddy has an extensive listing of stations in large cities, but fewer for small towns.

If you don't find your town listed at GasBuddy, don't dismay. You have several other choices. GasPriceWatch.com at www.gaspricewatch.com is a similar website that monitors gasoline prices all over the country. Its database currently has more than 130,000 stations. The site also offers easy ways to find the cheapest gas prices along the way as you travel.

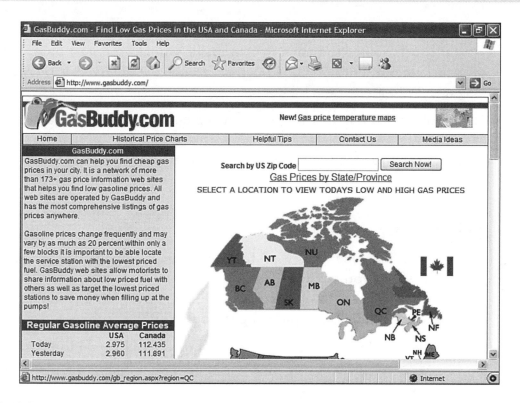

FIGURE 5.13
The GasBuddy website tracks gasoline prices around the country.

Both GasBuddy and GasPriceWatch.com use "spotters"—volunteers who enter the gasoline prices in their neighborhoods. People write down the gas prices of stations they frequent or that they see in their daily wanderings. Then they log on to these websites and post the prices for everyone to see. This works surprisingly well, because people are always excited to share any bargains they find. It is also enjoyable to help steer others away from overpriced stations.

The AAA Motor Club also offers a Fuel Price Finder at http://aaa. opisnet.com. It derives its gasoline prices from credit card transactions at more than 85,000 service stations and direct feeds from individual gasoline chains. The site displays the last price received and the date it was received. Unfortunately, the AAA online service is tied to the local

AAA websites. Therefore, often when you try to use it for the first time, it transports you to the main AAA website, where you must enter your zip code and then click Fuel Price Finder. The service is free, but gaining access to it can be a bit confusing.

Last but not least in the low-price-finding category is the Motor Trend Find Cheap Gas website at www.motortrend.com/gas_prices/index.html. This website had the most gas stations listed for Pinehurst, NC, the small town where I live.

Navigation and Maps

Chapter 2, "Planning Your Trip," touched on mapping websites. Because knowing where you are and where you're going is so important when you are on the road, I want to talk a little more about the wonders of online maps and global positioning systems (GPSs).

The easiest way to find your way around when you are on the road is with a GPS, which uses satellites to pinpoint your location and give you visual and/or verbal directions.

The best tip I can give you about GPSs is to thoroughly investigate the system before your purchase. I have used some systems that took so long to pinpoint my location that I was at my destination before they figured out where I was. I have also used a few whose built-in maps were neither up-to-date nor accurate. Price is not necessarily an indication of quality when it comes to GPSs, so you need to do some careful shopping.

LINGO

GPS stands for *global positioning system*. This is a navigation system formed by 24 satellites orbiting the earth that can read the exact location of a GPS receiver.

When you buy a new vehicle, you usually get only one GPS to choose from as a dealer-installed option. Check it out before you sign on the dotted line. Remember that you can always install a different one after your purchase. Even some of those that mount on the windshield are adequate. As a matter of fact, one of my favorite in-car GPSs is the dash-mounted TomTom Go (www.tomtom.com.) The TomTom website gives you an overview of how a GPS works and offers a tour of how its various products work. Even if you don't purchase that brand, this is a good website to visit for an overview of how GPSs work.

New technologies are constantly emerging. Now you can even get GPS turn-by-turn instructions and maps on your cell phone. Several companies provide this instant navigation to cellular carriers such as Verizon. You must have a cell phone that supports it. Look for one that has a good color screen and good visibility in sunlight.

It is a little more difficult to enter addresses and navigate a map on a cell phone than on a dedicated GPS. And you pay an extra monthly fee, but you don't have to purchase a separate GPS device.

Even if you don't have a GPS, you can still get great navigational information on the Web. In fact, you may want to use both. Many GPSs help you plan your trip and give you points of interest along the way, but sometimes good mapping sites can be an additional resource.

Most mapping sites allow you to enter your starting point and destination. You can often also choose where you want to stay and sights you would like to see. When your trip is mapped, you can print the maps and directions, or you can transfer that information to your laptop computer. In some cases, you can even transfer it to a handheld unit such as a Palm Personal Digital Assistant.

The "Mapping Sites" section in Chapter 2 contained a short list of online mapping websites. Here I list those plus a few more. Look at each. Check out the interface and see how easy (or difficult) it is to use. You may even want to create a few maps and take a short trip across town or a weekend jaunt to check out their accuracy before your cross-country tour.

BLOOPER ALERT

If you print maps from the Internet, be sure to check their accuracy by comparing maps from several different websites. It is often difficult to tell just how current or accurate the Internet mapping sites are.

- Google Maps: http://maps.google.com

- MapBlast! (MSN Maps): http://maps.msn.com

- MapsOnUs: www.mapsonus.com

- Maporama: http://world.maporama.com

- MapQuest: www.mapquest.com

- Michelin Route Planner: www.viamichelin.com/viamichelin/
  gbr/tpl/hme/MaHomePage.htm (driving directions in
  Europe)

- Mile by Mile: www.milebymile.com

- Yahoo! Maps: http://maps.yahoo.com

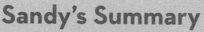

Sandy's Summary

Ever since Henry Ford produced his first automobile, the lure of the road has enticed drivers and passengers everywhere.

The Internet is a wonderful tool for blacktop wanderers. It can help you find destinations and plan road trips.

If a love of motorcycles rubbed off on you from James Dean, Fonzie, or your uncle Fred, the Internet is a great resource for you. You can see classic motorcycles in a variety of online motorcycle museums, get information on motorcycle events and rides, and even check out the helmet laws in every state.

You also want to be sure your car is in tip-top shape before you head out on that cross-country trek. Be sure to visit the car care sites for extra help with repairing and maintaining your vehicle.

Whether you are a dedicated RVer or are renting one for the first time, Internet resources are a valuable addition to your trip tools. You can find advice from other RVers, plan trips, locate campgrounds, and even get purchasing advice.

Technology really comes to your aid when you get on the road and need to find the best route. Both GPSs and online mapping sites are extraordinary resources for finding your way around.

So check out those online resources before you get on the road, and happy motoring!

Sandy Berger

Chapter 6

Distinctive Travel Adventures

Like all great travelers, I have seen more than I remember, and remember more than I have seen.

—Benjamin Disraeli

o you find yourself gravitating to the same places when you are planning a vacation? Vacations don't have to be repetitive unless you want them to be. Sometimes it is fun to spice up your life by trying a different type of vacation. If you have always vacationed at the beach, why not try the mountains? Spend most of your travel time in an RV? Why not try a cruise?

Better yet, let the Internet be your guide to some unique adventures. Whether you want an adventurous vacation such as shark diving, or you prefer a relaxing stay at a lovely bed-and-breakfast, there is something for everyone.

In This Chapter

- Offbeat Adventures
- Follow the Stars
- Spas and Wellness Vacations
- Sports and Outdoor Recreation
- Bed-and-Breakfasts
- Vacations Tailored to Boomers and Beyond
- Traveling Alone
- The Next Adventure: Space Travel

Offbeat Adventures

Whether you have always looked for something different, or you are tired of the same old travel experiences, many distinctive and unique adventures are waiting for you.

You can always start with something you love and turn it into an exciting vacation. If cooking is your forte, why not take cooking lessons in Tuscany, attend a two-week language and culinary program in France, or sign up for Le Cordon Bleu in Japan? The Shaw Guides to Recreational Cooking & Wine Schools at http://cookforfun.shawguides.com is filled with great ideas.

Also check out the other guides at www.shawguides.com for arts and crafts workshops, tennis and golf schools, photography workshops, and language vacations, as shown in Figure 6.1.

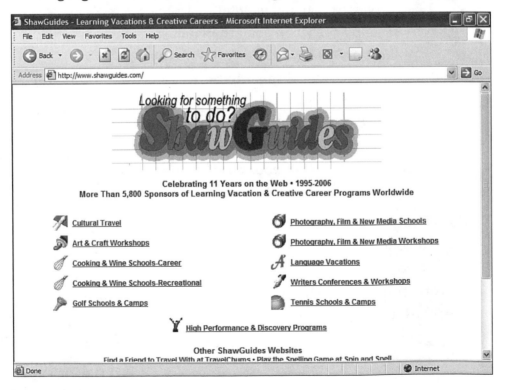

FIGURE 6.1
The ShawGuides website is filled with vacation ideas for enjoying your hobby or craft.

If your tastes lean a little more toward the cultural, you can learn about art, history, and architecture by visiting sites of interest around the world. There are more historic sites and architectural wonders than you can imagine.

The InfoHub Specialty Travel Guide at www.infohub.com gives you plenty of ideas. Learn about the pyramids or the Wailing Wall. Satisfy your curiosity by learning about historic events while actually visiting the sites. This website lets you view details about its vacations or order free brochures directly from its suppliers. You'll will find ideas for places you never knew existed.

If you love to garden, you might also consider a garden tour of the British Isles, Northern Europe, or even Africa. The Gardenvisit.com website at www.gardenvisit.com gives you numerous ideas for garden tours as well as garden touring advice for various countries.

If you would like to learn something while on vacation, check out Smithsonian Journeys at www.smithsonianjourneys.org, shown in Figure 6.2. Smithsonian Journeys is known for the best in educational travel. From international travel to short journeys here in the U.S., the Smithsonian Journeys website gives you ideas for travel learning at its best.

But maybe you don't have a hobby or a burning interest and you aren't interested in a learning vacation. If you are the type who joined the Peace Corps in the '60s, or at least wanted to, perhaps a volunteer vacation would be perfect for you. TripSpot has an area focused on volunteer travel at www.tripspot.com/features/volunteertravel.htm. This site has ideas and links for all types of vacations where you can spend your time improving the environment and communities of countries all over the world. Although many organizations are covered here, you may also want to consider volunteering for organizations such as the Red Cross (www.redcross.org) or Habitat for Humanity (www.habitat.org), which are always looking for volunteers.

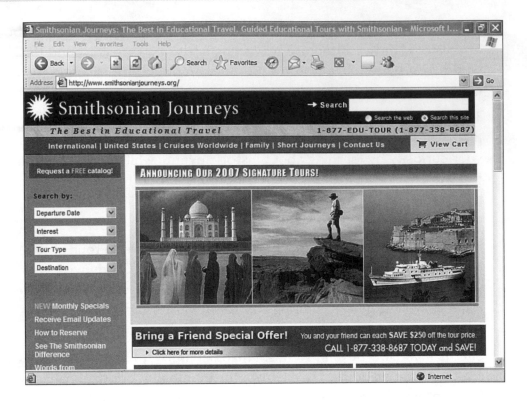

FIGURE 6.2
The Smithsonian Journeys website features some of the best in educational travel.

Perhaps you have always wanted to have a religious experience. But do you know how and where to get tickets to see the Pope? Don't worry—the Internet has all the answers. For a Papal audience, visit the Church of Santa Susanna, home of the American Catholic Church in Rome, at www.santasusanna.org/popeVatican/tickets.html. As shown in Figure 6.3, this site has information on getting an audience with the Pope, as well as information on the Pope and the Vatican. If you are interested in visiting the Vatican, you can find more information at the official Vatican website at www.vatican.va.

BLOOPER ALERT

Be sure to type in Web addresses exactly as they are given. www.vatican.com takes you to a different place than the suggested www.vatican.va.

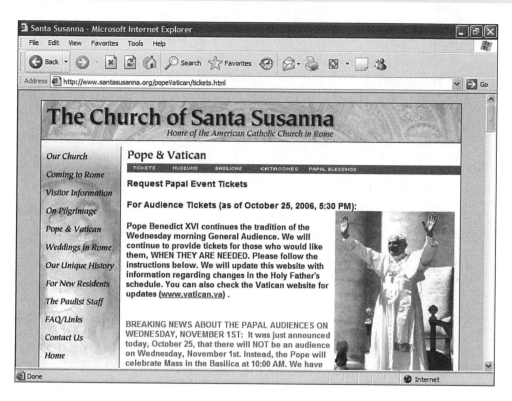

FIGURE 6.3
On this website you can get tickets to see the Pope.

Follow the Stars

Want a truly luxurious vacation? Why not follow the stars? A little Internet research will turn up vacation spots that celebrities often visit. These are places that the likes of Oprah Winfrey, Bill Gates, and Warren Buffett have enjoyed. The MSN MoneyCentral website (http://moneycentral.msn.com/content/invest/forbes/P62432.asp) lists the top 10 places:

- The Wakaya Club, Fiji Islands: www.wakaya.com

- The Inn at Langley, Langley, Washington: www.innatlangley.com

- Longhouse, Waiheke Island, New Zealand

- The Pink Beach Club, Bermuda: www.pinkbeach.com

- The Greenbrier, White Sulphur Springs, West Virginia: www.greenbrier.com

- The Maidstone Arms, East Hampton, New York: www.maidstonearms.com

- The Big EZ Lodge, Big Sky, Montana: www.bigezlodge.com

- Half Moon Gold Tennis & Beach Club, Montego Bay: www.halfmoon.com

- The Breakers, Palm Beach, Florida: www.thebreakers.com

- The Bacara Resort & Spa, Santa Barbara, California: www.bacararesort.com

You may want to check out a few of these luxury resort websites just to see the site content and the photographs.

If you've been saving your money and you decide to visit one of these, or other celebrity hot spots, you may just be lucky enough to encounter a celebrity. For example, Oprah Winfrey recently purchased a 46-acre estate in Santa Barbara, California. You may recognize the names of a few of her neighbors, including Julia Child, Brad Pitt, and Julia Louis-Dreyfus. So if you are looking for celebrities, you may look for a Santa Barbara vacation. Other celebrity hotspots include Aspen, Colorado and Hawaii.

Seeing celebrities while on vacation can be exciting. I know because I'll never forget having seen Elizabeth Taylor and Richard Burton at a resort in Hawaii. It was obviously years ago, but it's something I'll always remember.

If you just want a feeling of luxury while on vacation, follow the ideas in the MSNBC Luxury Travel area at www.msnbc.msn.com/id/6845110. They tell you where to get the world's most expensive steaks; how to book the high-roller suites in Las Vegas; and how Oprah, Cruise, and other celebrities fly. For a truly luxurious vacation you may also want to visit Luxury Link at www.luxurylink.com, which specializes in luxury travel options. Follow the suggestions, and you are in for a truly pampered vacation.

Spas and Wellness Vacations

To continue talking about pampered vacations, one of the most popular types of unique vacations today are spa and wellness vacations.

The Well Traveled Tours website at www.welltraveledtours.com promises that "You'll embark on a journey of a lifetime. You'll come home with far more than photos. You'll return with a healthier, more balanced approach to life and how to live it, once-in-a-lifetime memories, and new friends in places near and far." Many companies like this are taking a holistic approach to wellness and combining that with travel. For many this is the best of both worlds.

For more information on this new type of vacation, check out the Travel to Wellness website at www.traveltowellness.com. As shown in Figure 6.4, Travel to Wellness has links to Wellness Vacations, Wellness Festivals, and Girl Getaways, as well as lists of different types of spas and how to find them.

FIGURE 6.4
The Travel to Wellness website has a variety of information on spas and wellness vacations.

Sports and Outdoor Recreation

After investigating pampered vacation ideas, perhaps you are ready for a different kind of vacation—one where you can get your blood pumping.

Sports and outdoor vacations have always been popular. Baby boomers are still enjoying the outdoors as they did in their younger years. Even backpacking is still popular, although now we may use the Internet to find the hostels (www.hostels.com) that we used to find by hiking from town to town.

If you've passed your backpacking years, other active travel options are available. From golf getaways to alpine adventures, we are still ready to be on the move.

Perhaps you've gone golfing in Myrtle Beach, South Carolina or Pinehurst, North Carolina. Maybe you've skied the slopes of Aspen or Vail. You are looking for some new ideas, and the Internet does not disappoint. It has a myriad of ideas for active travel. Here are just a few:

- Country Walkers: www.countrywalkers.com. Has walking tours and hiking vacations of varying lengths in areas from historic villages to exotic jungles.

- Cycle Europe: www.cycle-europe.com. An exciting guide to cycling in Europe. It's even good for cycling spectators.

- Alpine Huts: www.initaly.com/travel/info/alpine.htm. A guide to mountain district huts in Italy.

- Cicerone Guidebooks: www.cicerone.co.uk. Guide books for walkers, trekkers, mountaineers, climbers, and cyclists, especially focused on the British Isles and Europe.

- The Trail Database: www.traildatabase.org. The world's largest hiking trail database, covering many parts of the world.

- Great Outdoor Recreation Pages: http://gorp.com. Tips and activity guides for hiking, biking, climbing, fishing, skiing, and just about any other outdoor sport or activity.

- GoSki: www.goski.com. Covers more than 2,000 ski resorts in more than 37 countries.

- Tennis Resorts Online: www.tennisresortsonline.com. A guide to the world's best tennis resorts and tennis camps. The brainchild of veteran tennis writer Roger Cox.

- Linkaway Golf: www.linkaway.com. More than 3,300 golf-related links in 90 different countries.

If there are still some adventures on your life's to-do list, check out the Mountain Travel Sobek Adventure Company website at www.mountaintravelsobek.com. From trekking in the Himalayas to exploring exotic areas such as Patagonia in South America, you may just find the fulfilling vacation you've always dreamed of.

Austin-Lehman Adventures (www.austinlehman.com) also helps you find the adventure vacation of your dreams. It has biking, hiking, climbing, paddling, equestrian, and swimming adventures for everyone from a single to a family.

Some companies combine luxury and exercise. For instance, the Butterfield & Roginson website at www.butterfield.com has passenger yachts that take you to exotic locations for biking and walking tours with some of the best scenery in the world.

Don't overlook the many unique sporting vacations that can be found on the Internet. For instance, the Shark Diver website (www.shark-diver.com), shown in Figure 6.5, leads you on a safe shark-diving and giant-squid adventure.

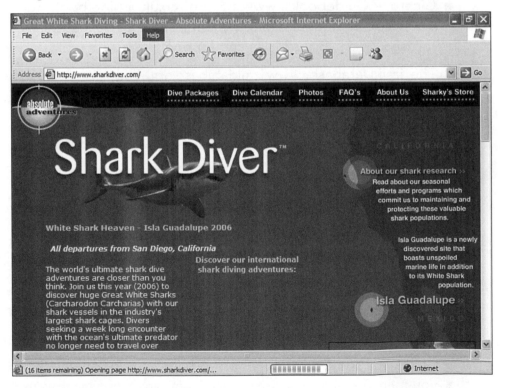

FIGURE 6.5
The Shark Diver website gives you the ultimate shark-dive adventure.

Bed-and-Breakfasts

If you don't like sleeping in a tent, but you don't find large hotels appealing either, perhaps you would enjoy a bed-and-breakfast vacation.

In days gone by, it was not unusual for country travelers to spend the night at private houses. That is how the idea of a bed-and-breakfast began. These are private residences with several rooms set aside as paid accommodations for guests. Because the homeowners generally included breakfast, these homes became known as bed-and-breakfasts.

Often today's bed-and-breakfasts are located in attractive older houses that have been renovated but maintain their unique antique character. Sometimes, the entire home is rented to guests.

B&Bs are generally found in historic towns and villages, but even large cities such as London, New York, and Chicago have their share of bed-and-breakfast lodgings.

Innkeepers of this type have found that the Internet is a great way to market their wares, and visitors who love the homey feel use the Internet to find the most comfortable accommodations.

You can often find bed-and-breakfast accommodations by looking at directories for the location where you will be staying, but it is often easiest to find them at some of the many bed-and-breakfast sites on the Web. The following are some of the more popular.

The Bed and Breakfast Connector at www.bbconnector.com lists quality bed-and-breakfast lodgings for the United States and Canada, as shown in Figure 6.6. Some have photos and links to the innkeeper's website. All have telephone numbers.

At BnBstar.com (www.BnBStar.com) you can look up bed-and-breakfasts by city, area, or zip code for the United States, Canada, and the UK. You can also find B&Bs that have specials for honeymooning couples, skiers, and gay couples. This site also features large Victorian inns and lists B&Bs that have been inspected by the Innkeepers Association.

FIGURE 6.6
The Bed and Breakfast Connector has pictures of many inns.

Here are some other sites for finding bed-and-breakfasts:

- Pamela Lanier's Bed and Breakfasts: www.lanierbb.com

- Bed & Breakfast Inns Online: www.bbonline.com

- BedandBreakfast.com: www.bedandbreakfast.com

- Pillows and Pancakes.com: www.pillowsandpancakes.com

- IBBP: www.ibbp.com

The IBBP website provides listings for Australia, New Zealand, the UK, Mexico, Italy, France, the Netherlands, Spain, Canada, and Africa as well as the United States.

Vacations Tailored to Boomers and Beyond

If you are a baby boomer, you probably remember the time when it seemed like everyone was trying to create a product you would like. There was Ovaltine to drink, the *Howdy Doody Show* to watch, and Brylcream for your hair.

For awhile it seemed that the marketers forgot about the boomers, but now they are again starting to create packages and products for us. When you see how many travel websites are geared to the older generation, you will feel right at home.

The trend is slowly shifting away from family-oriented vacations to adults-only vacations. There is much to choose from. Many groups and websites have offerings for those over 50.

Statistics show that, of all the countries in the world, Canada has the biggest percentage of baby boomers. So it is not surprising that Canada is one of the first countries to grab this trend and run with it. Some vacation spots in Canada, such as the Heather Lodge (www.heather-lodge.com) in the Haliburton Highlands of Ontario, are gearing up for boomers. They offer full-service resorts with spa services and home-cooked meals. Canadian resorts are moving to the adults-only trend to appeal to vacationers who want a peaceful vacation spot (without screaming children or harried parents). In addition, they are realizing that boomers love a bargain, so they are trying to offer quality service at affordable prices.

Although you can find individual accommodations like this by searching the Web, many websites help make your search more efficient by listing the vacations, adventures, and expeditions that they feel are attractive to the over-50 crowd.

The Frommer's website has an area for mature travelers at www.frommers.com/trip_ideas/senior. It features a trip-planning resource guide for seniors that can be accessed as shown in Figure 6.7. It also includes information on discounts for seniors.

Trip Planning Resources

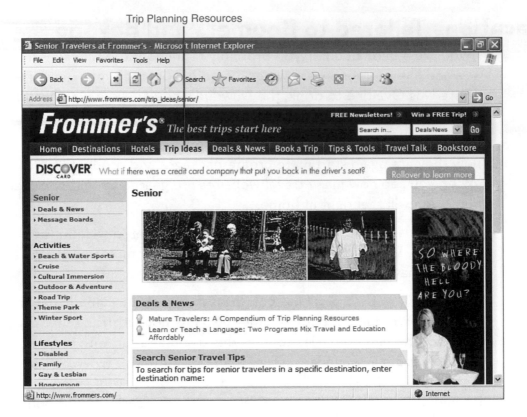

FIGURE 6.7
The Frommer's website lists trip-planning resources and discounts for seniors.

The Elderhostel website is dedicated to learning adventures for active seniors. It is a not-for-profit group that offers travel adventures that include history, culture, nature, music, walking, biking, crafts, and study cruises. Elderhostel has programs in the U.S. and Canada as well as international programs. Its most popular adventures include a cruise down the Seine to the D-day beaches, the Clinton Presidential Library, and a trip to France to study the French Impressionists and the School of Barbizon. This website also includes plenty of free information and ideas.

Eldertreks, at www.eldertreks.com, is the world's first adventure travel company designed exclusively for people 50 and over. It offers off-the-beaten-path adventures in more than 80 countries. It can help you plan a wildlife safari in Tanzania, an exploratory trip to Papua New Guinea, or a hiking journey to Tibet's holy mountains of Mt. Kailash and Mt. Everest. Although some of the treks are rugged adventures, Eldertreks offers interesting adventures for the mild-hearted as well.

The Wired Seniors Network has a Seniors Travel Guide website at http://seniorstravelguide.com. It features adventure travel such as dude ranches and safaris, but it also has links to home exchanges, bed-and-breakfasts, fishing lodges, and just about every type of vacation that those over 50 may be interested in. It even provides links to Ecotourism and travel services, and destination guides, all geared toward older adults.

The China Hiking Adventures website at www.china-hiking.com is aimed at seniors who want to tour China.

The Smarter Living Senior Travel website, at www.smarterliving.com/senior, has information on senior discounts for hotels, airfare, car rentals, and cruises. You'll find many discounts and tempting deals. You can sign up for the free Senior Travel Newsletter to get last-minute travel discounts.

The Travel with a Challenge Web magazine (www.travelwithachallenge.com) features countries, cultures, cruises, and nature vacations for mature travelers. Its travel articles are unique and interesting.

The Walking the World website (www.walkingtheworld.com) with Ward Luthi features travel adventures for those over 50. Whether you are interested in walking through small villages or majestic forests, Luthi helps you plan your trip.

Here are some other websites you may want to peruse for ideas on travel for seniors:

- 50+ Expeditions: www.50plusexpeditions.com
- Smartertravel.com: www.smartertravel.com/senior-travel

- ElderTrav.com: www.eldertrav.com

- Adventures Abroad: www.adventuresabroad.com/category/gold-enyears.jsp

Traveling Alone

Not having a travel companion is no longer a good reason to stay home. Many websites help men and women who are traveling alone. Often travel costs are based on double-occupancy rooms for two people. If you travel alone, there is an additional cost called a single supplement cost. For ideas on avoiding that single supplement cost and advice on traveling alone, visit the Connecting Solo Travel Network at www.cstn.org. Its theme is "Travel Alone, Not Lonely," and it offers tips on how to do that.

The Travel Insider at www.thetravelinsider.info/2002/0802.htm also has valuable tips on traveling alone.

JourneyWoman.com (www.journeywoman.com) has excellent articles on travel for the adventurous woman over 50. It has ideas and tips for fun travel for women on their own.

If you are a woman traveling alone, check out the Tips for Women Traveling Alone at the U.S. Department of State website at http://travel.state.gov/travel/tips/brochures/brochures_1227.html. They clue you in on some of the problems that women traveling alone can encounter in foreign countries. Two of the examples are that it is illegal in Laos to invite Lao nationals of the opposite sex to your hotel room and that foreigners in Saudi Arabia have been arrested for "improper dress." Reading this could help make your trip pleasantly uneventful.

If you are traveling alone, don't forget spas, which are great for both men and women. You can structure your daily plan to do the things you love, and it's easy to meet other singles.

The Next Adventure: Space Travel

Have you ever dreamed of becoming an astronaut? Well, you may get your chance. In the past, space flight has been reserved for highly trained astronauts or cosmonauts who dedicated their lives to their mission. But now, the journey into the wild blue yonder may be opening up to the average person.

Here's how it happened. In 2004 a three-person aircraft named SpaceShipOne won a $10 million prize for being flown into space, 62 miles above the Earth. Burt Rutan, who developed SpaceShipOne, has teamed with Richard Branson of Virgin Galactic to design a larger craft capable of carrying up to five passengers into space. It will be designed to hold passengers and give them an extraordinary view from space.

The trip will be pricey, especially for the first passengers, who are lining up to pay up to $200,000 for a round-trip ticket. If you are looking for a truly unique adventure, get out your pocketbook and make your reservation.

Sandy's Summary

Vacations don't have to be mundane. With the help of Internet resources, they never will be. Some trips will be offbeat adventures, and others will be learning experiences, but all are sure to be exciting.

Start with something you love. Whether it's cooking, gardening, or art, the Internet can help you find ideas and resources to turn your love into a travel adventure.

You don't have to use the websites I've mentioned to book your trip. In fact, I don't want you to do that until you have thoroughly investigated your options. But the websites described in this chapter will help open your mind and give you great vacation ideas.

Whether you want to visit the Pope or hobnob with celebrities, unique vacations are available for everyone. They may include sports or exercise, or they may just consist of lounging around a bed-and-breakfast. Whatever you like, with a little online help, you can turn it into the vacation of your dreams.

Sandy Berger

Chapter 7

International Travel

Most travel is best of all in the anticipation or the remembering; the reality has more to do with losing your luggage.

—Regina Nadelson

The world is at your fingertips—literally, thanks to the Internet. Travel abroad can be mind-broadening and exciting, but it always requires a little more preparation than domestic travel. Abundant Internet resources can help you get ready for your international travel.

International Travel Tips

Whether you are planning your first trip abroad or you are a seasoned traveler of the world, it always pays to get tips from the experts, and the Internet makes this easy.

The people at the U.S. State Department have a lot of experience with traveling to foreign lands. They also have a lot of experience keeping Americans out of trouble as they visit abroad. So I'll leave it to the experts and list the U.S. State Department's top 10 tips to make your trip easier:

1. Make sure you have a signed, valid passport and visas, if required. Also, before you go, fill in your passport's emergency information page!

2. Make two copies of your passport identification page. This will facilitate replacement if your passport is lost or stolen. Leave one copy at home with friends or relatives. Carry the other with you in a place separate from your passport.

3. Leave a detailed copy of your itinerary with family or friends at home so that you can be contacted in case of an emergency. Also leave the numbers or copies of your passport or other citizenship documents.

4. Prior to your departure, register with the nearest U.S. embassy or consulate through the State Department's travel registration website at https://travelregistration.state.gov/ibrs. Registration makes your presence and whereabouts known in case someone needs to contact you in an emergency. In accordance with the Privacy Act, information on your welfare and whereabouts may not be released without your express authorization.

5. Read the Consular Information Sheets (and Public Announcements or Travel Warnings, if applicable) for the countries you plan to visit.

6. Do not leave your luggage unattended in public areas. Do not accept packages from strangers.

7. To avoid being a target of crime, try not to wear conspicuous clothing or expensive jewelry, and do not carry excessive amounts of money or unnecessary credit cards.

8. Familiarize yourself with the local laws and customs of the countries to which you are traveling. Remember, the U.S. Constitution does not follow you! While in a foreign country, you are subject to its laws.

9. To avoid violating local laws, deal only with authorized agents when you exchange money or purchase art or antiques.

10. If you get into trouble, contact the nearest U.S. embassy.

You can find a copy of these tips and more valuable information at http://travel. state.gov/travel/tips/tips_1232.html. The State Department also has many other tips on traveling abroad. Just surf to Travel.State.Gov at http://travel.state.gov and click International Travel, as shown in Figure 7.1.

sandy's tip
When traveling abroad, always take the telephone number and address of your country's embassy with you.

The CIA World Factbook, which can be found at www.cia.gov/cia/ publications/factbook, is an informative online reference book that was created by the U.S. Central Intelligence Agency. This online book is updated continually and holds information about every country on the planet. Although it has some dry statistics, it also has information that can be valuable to the international traveler.

The drop-down menu has a list of choices that include more than 260 countries, from Afghanistan to Zimbabwe. Choose the country of your choice, and you are given statistics including history, geography, population, government, economy, and transportation. This is a valuable resource for international travelers who want to be informed travelers.

FIGURE 7.1
The U.S. Department of State has a wealth of information about international travel at its Travel.State.Gov website.

For more tips on international travel, you may want to visit World Travel Tips at www.worldtraveltips.net. As shown in Figure 7.2, you simply choose the country you are interested in.

You are taken to a site with information about that country, including statistics such as time zone, population, languages, power, currency, and climate. Major cities are also listed, along with tips about laws, public transportation, and other useful information. World Travel Tips is also a community website you can join. You can discuss your experiences in different countries of the world with others who are interested in the same locations.

FIGURE 7.2
The World Travel Tips website has information on just about any country in the world.

On the bottom of the page for each country you see links to members who live in that country, members postings about that country, and member tips for that country.

The Free Travel Tips.com website also has a research links page at www.freetraveltips.com/Links. This area has useful links to everything for travelers, from getting medical attention to finding Internet access.

If you will be traveling through Europe, it's good to get advice from a seasoned traveler. Rick Steves, who has taught smart European travel for 30 years, is a great resource. Check out his Rick Steves' Europe Through the Back Door website at www.ricksteves.com, shown in Figure 7.3. Steves helps you plan your trip and gives you travel news. You can also listen to his free podcasts, where he talks about travel in Europe.

FIGURE 7.3
Rick Steves shares his wealth of knowledge about traveling in Europe on his website.

Sandy's tip
Use the Internet to do research for your travels. Learn as much as you can about your destination before you leave home. That way, you are ready for just about any situation when you arrive at your destination.

When you are looking for information on preparing for a trip abroad, you won't want to miss the TravelSense website at www.travelsense.org. This website was developed and is run by the American Society of Travel Agents. Although it does not have a specific area on international travel, it is filled with tips and information about travel hot spots around the world. It also has plenty of information for U.S. citizens traveling abroad.

Special Requirements for International Travel

Often special paperwork is required to enter and leave a foreign country. The U.S. Department of State at http://travel. state.gov is the best spot for information on the necessary passports and visas. It also lists services that are available for U.S. citizens abroad. Special note should also be taken of travel warnings that have been issued for your destination.

BLOOPER ALERT

Make sure your passport is valid. If it is near expiration, have it renewed, because some countries will consider it invalid if it is too close to expiration.

To get to the passport area of the Travel.State.Gov website, simply choose Passports from the horizontal menu. If you need information on obtaining a visa, click the word Visas, which is the next menu choice. These two areas tell you everything you need to know about getting or renewing a passport or visa.

Through normal processes, it can take a month or two to get a passport or have one renewed. So be sure to start the process as soon as you can. Getting a visa can take even longer, because that is done through the country you plan to visit.

If you need your passport in a hurry, the U.S. Passport Service Guide at www.us-passport-service-guide.com/directory helps you expedite the process. I used this site when I needed my passport renewed quickly, and it got me my passport in seven days. You pay extra for this service, but when you need a passport quickly, it is definitely worth the price. This site can also expedite visas and other necessary travel papers.

More useful information on entry requirements for various countries is available at the Frommer's Entry Requirements & Customs area at www.frommers.com/tips/entry_requirements_and_customs.

Language and Customs

In many parts of the world, English is spoken and understood, but it is always good to have at least rudimentary knowledge of the language of the country you will be visiting. Learning a few useful words and phrases before your trip can go a long way toward making your trip more enjoyable.

Again, Internet resources can help. The Living Language section at www.fodors.com/language has a wide variety of useful expressions in French, German, Italian, and Spanish. You can choose from any of the useful areas, which include useful expressions, at the airport, accommodations, dining out, shopping, health care, and more. As shown in Figure 7.4, you simply choose the language and then choose the area. You are presented with a large collection of useful expressions, along with a pronunciation guide. If you click any word or expression, the program pronounces it for you.

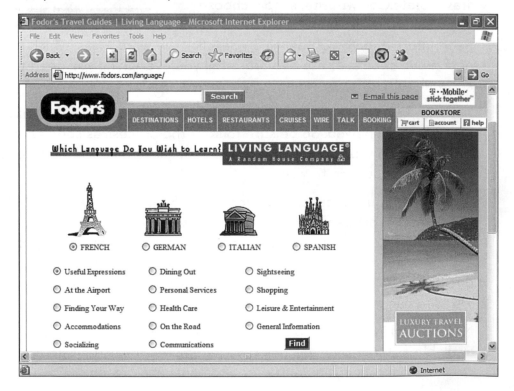

FIGURE 7.4
The Fodor's free Living Language site helps you learn and pronounce simple expressions in several languages.

If you are practicing a language and you need help with translation, check out the Babel Fish Translation page at http://babelfish.altavista. digital.com. Enter a block of text, and it gets translated into a variety of languages, including Dutch, Greek, Italian, Korean, Portuguese, and many more.

If you need help with a different language, just type the language and the word "translator" or "translation" into any search engine, and you will find plenty of help.

Don't forget that many different handheld devices are now available that can help you learn a foreign language. They also can be useful for a quick translation on the road.

When you are in a foreign country, remember that its customs may be very different. It is best to learn all you can about that country and its customs before you leave home.

Everything can be different in the country you will visit. The people speak a different language and have different currency and different electricity. For information on any country, check out Wikipedia at http://en.wikipedia.com. Wikipedia is a free online encyclopedia that is updated and added to by ordinary people.

Wikipedia can tell you the history, politics, geography, and economy of any country. You also can learn about the culture and customs. Be sure to read as much as you can about the country you will visit. For example, the Wikipedia article about Greece is shown in Figure 7.5. When you get near the bottom of the page, you see a section called "External links." The first listings give official links that include the national tourism organization and other useful information.

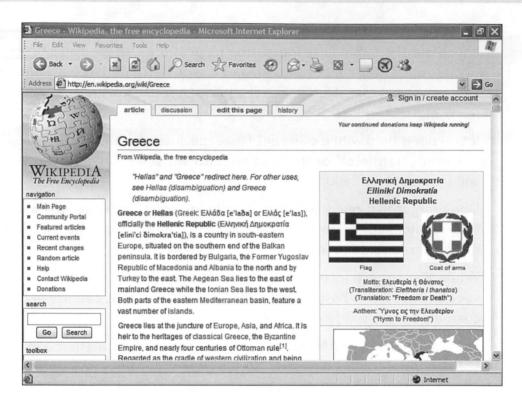

FIGURE 7.5
The free Wikipedia online encyclopedia gives you information on just about any country. The information on Greece is shown here.

Health and Insurance

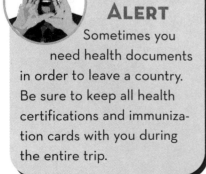

BLOOPER ALERT

Sometimes you need health documents in order to leave a country. Be sure to keep all health certifications and immunization cards with you during the entire trip.

Find out what types of diseases are common to the country you will be visiting, and be sure to get all the necessary vaccinations and take all the necessary precautions. You might need to take medications before, during, and after your trip, so be sure to start researching the health problems of your destination early. Internet research can be valuable here, but it is always wise to check with your primary care physician for details.

It is especially important when traveling abroad to check your medical insurance to see what type of coverage you may have when you are in a foreign country. If necessary, consider purchasing special insurance for the trip.

More information on health and travel insurance can be found at many of the websites mentioned in this book. The Frommer's website has some excellent information at www.frommers.com/tips/health_and_travel_insurance/.

Driving in a Foreign Country

Remember that driving a car in a foreign country can be a very foreign experience. In some countries people drive on the left side of the road, some go counterclockwise around traffic circles (roundabouts), and some have rules of the road that may seem totally out of the ordinary to us (some seem to have no rules at all!). So if you are planning to drive in a foreign country, you will want to use Internet resources to check out the local driving regulations. Also check out the road signs, which may look very different from American road signs. Often information of this type is available from the country's national tourism website.

BLOOPER ALERT
Some countries have both a minimum and maximum age you must be to rent a car. Be sure to check carefully.

Also keep in mind the following:

- You might need to obtain an international driver's license or need special insurance.

- If you will rent a car, you need to check out the rules and what you need to have with you well in advance of the trip.

- You may have to pay a permit fee that allows you to drive in that country.

- Some countries with modern highways allow much higher speeds than in the U.S. Therefore, it is especially important to stay out of the fast lane unless you are passing or are willing to travel at these high rates of speed.

- Your personal automobile insurance may not be valid in the country you are visiting. If you need additional coverage, purchase it from your insurance company or the car rental company.

- If you can't drive a stick shift, make sure you rent a car with an automatic transmission. Many foreign rental fleets have only a few automatic cars.

Sandy's Summary

Traveling to foreign lands can be both interesting and exciting, but journeys of this type require more preparation than domestic trips.

First, you should investigate the passport, visa, and other paperwork that may be required. You will also want to check out the types of vaccinations and other medical precautions you might need. All this can take time, so be sure to start the process early.

You will also want to learn all you can about the country you will visit, including a little about the language and customs. Internet resources will help you with your quest for information about any country in the world.

You will also want to prepare well in advance if you want to rent a car or drive in a foreign country.

With travel abroad, a little preparation can go a long way toward helping you have an enjoyable and stress-free trip.

Sandy Berger

Chapter 8

Healthy Travel and Special Needs

Travel and change of place impart new vigor to the mind.

—Seneca

Your good health is one of your most important assets. You guard it in everyday living, and you must also protect it when you are traveling. When traveling overseas you may need vaccinations and medications that you don't need when traveling domestically. As usual, the Internet comes through with information on what's needed for each country. You can also surf the Web to find what to put in your travel first aid kit and how to prepare for travel if you or a companion are disabled.

In This Chapter

- Safeguarding Your Health
- Supporting Travelers with Special Needs
- Traveling with Children

Safeguarding Your Health

Sometimes the most reasonable, commonsense practices are the ones most often overlooked when you are on vacation or on the road. This often happens because we travel to destinations that are foreign to us.

Sandy's tip

Read travel blogs and message boards to learn about the health-related experiences of others who have visited the location you will visit. Often this can help you prevent or prepare for potential problems.

For example, most people remember to use extra sun protection when they visit tropical areas, but they may not realize that this is also necessary for ski resorts.

You should always read as much as you can about your destination to determine what extra supplies you might need to take to protect your health. With Internet resources, it's easy to find this type of information.

Health Information for Your Destination at Travel Health Online

A great place to start is the Travel Health Online website at www.trip-prep.com. This website requires registration, but it is free. The website is easy to use, and it contains a wealth of information that travelers will find informative for protecting their health.

The Destination information of the Travel Health Online website, shown in Figure 8.1, covers destinations from Afghanistan to Zimbabwe and everything in between. The information for each country is invaluable for travelers. The status of the medical care in each country is detailed. The problem diseases and recommended and required vaccinations are listed. There is also information on insect-borne, and food and water-borne, diseases of the country. There is also information on weather and crime. In addition, the site lists each country's consular information, including the address, telephone number, and email address of the U.S. and Canadian Embassies.

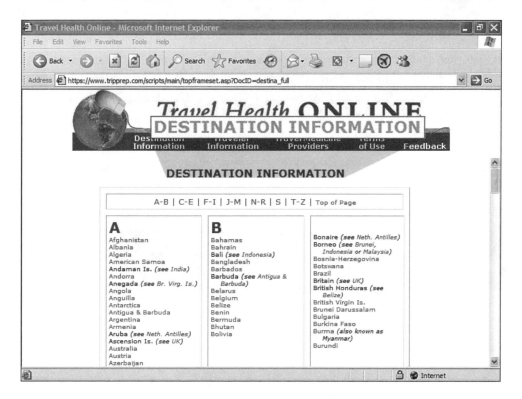

FIGURE 8.1
The Destination Information section of the Travel Health Online website is a "don't miss" area for international travelers.

While you are at the Travel Health Online website, be sure to check out the Traveler Information and Travel Medicine Providers areas. The Traveler Information area provides data on everything from altitude illness to yellow fever. The Travel Medicine Providers area gives addresses and contact information for medical providers in the U.S. and countries around the world. The website states that the medical providers' information has not been verified nor their medical status reviewed, but in an emergency, it may be beneficial to have a medical contact, especially in a foreign country.

Advice from the Centers for Disease Control Website

When looking for health information for an upcoming trip, don't overlook the excellent information provided by the Department of Health and Human Services Centers for Disease Control (CDC) website at www.cdc.gov. Its Travelers' Health area (www.cdc.gov/travel), shown in Figure 8.2, is filled with useful health information.

FIGURE 8.2
The Travelers' Health area of the CDC website has valuable health information for travelers.

The Illness and Injury Abroad section of the CDC website at www.cdc.gov/travel/illness_injury_abroad.htm is a great resource for travelers who visit foreign countries. It covers travel-specific warnings but also has information on medical emergencies. Perhaps even more important is its information on planning for healthy travel and its tips on being prepared for health-related emergencies.

Even if you are not traveling abroad, you may want to visit the CDC website for its informative articles on healthy travel and its travel health kit information. This information, as shown in Figure 8.3, is in the Illness and Injury Abroad area at www.cdc.gov/travel/illness_injury_abroad.htm, but it is pertinent to all travelers.

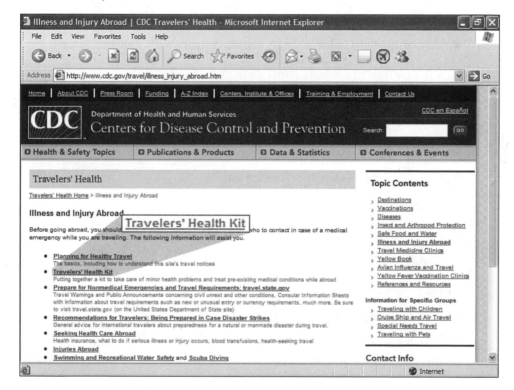

FIGURE 8.3
The Travelers' Health Kit recommended on the CDC website is useful for all travelers.

Here are the medications that the CDC recommends you take with you when you travel:

■ Personal prescription medications (also carry copies of all pre-scriptions, including the generic names of medications, and a note from the prescribing physician on his or her letterhead for con-trolled substances and injectable medications)

- Antimalarial medications, if applicable

- Antidiarrheal medication (such as bismuth subsalicylate or loperamide)

- Antibiotic for self-treatment of moderate to severe diarrhea

- Antihistamine

- Decongestant, alone or in combination with antihistamine

- Anti-motion-sickness medication

- Acetaminophen, aspirin, ibuprofen, or another medication for pain or fever

- Mild laxative

- Cough suppressant/expectorant

- Throat lozenges

- Antacid

- Antifungal and antibacterial ointments or creams

- 1% hydrocortisone cream

- Epinephrine auto-injector (such as EpiPen), especially if you have a history of severe allergic reaction. Also available in a smaller-dose package for children.

Here are some other important items that the CDC recommends:

- Insect repellent containing DEET (up to 50%)

- Sunscreen (preferably SPF 15 or greater)

- Aloe gel for sunburns

- Digital thermometer

- Oral rehydration solution packets

- Basic first-aid items (adhesive bandages, gauze, ace wrap, antiseptic, tweezers, scissors, cotton-tipped applicators)

- Antibacterial hand wipes or alcohol-based hand sanitizer

- Moleskin for blisters

- Lubricating eyedrops (such as Natural Tears)

- First-aid quick reference card

Every two years, the CDC produces the Yellow Book, which details health information for international travel. You can order this book, but it also is posted online free of charge. Even though the book is written for health-care providers, it uses fairly simple terminology and can be useful to any international traveler. Chapters include Pre and Post Travel Recommendations, Geographic Distribution of Potential Health Hazards to Travelers, Prevention of Specific Infectious Diseases, Yellow Fever Vaccine Requirements by Country, Conveyance and Transportation Issues, International Travel with Infants and Young Children, and Advising Travelers with Specific Needs.

Sandy's tip
To ensure your health care while on the road, you may want to bring a copy of your health records along when you travel. This is of particular importance to anyone with chronic health problems.

As noted in the CDC travelers' list, don't forget to take sunscreen. Also remember simple things like warm clothing for cold areas and sun-protective clothing for sunny places. Although layering your clothing to keep warm is always a good idea, today you can find artificially heated clothing.

For clothing with built-in sun protection, see websites such as Coolibar (www.coolibar.com), shown in Figure 8.4. This Australian company creates soft, pliable clothing that blocks the sun's burning rays.

Sandy's tip
Before leaving your own country, be sure to purchase health insurance that will cover you in the event of a medical emergency.

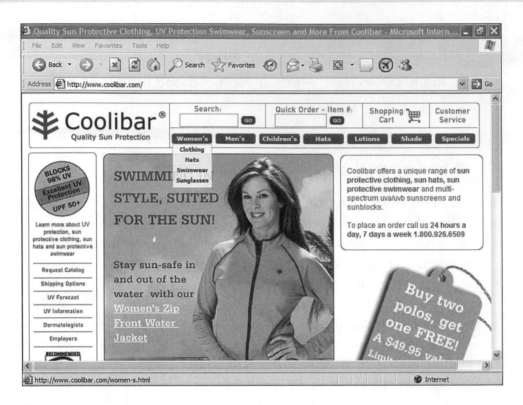

FIGURE 8.4
The Coolibar website provides soft, comfortable, sun-protective clothing.

Sandy's tip

Take along extra prescriptions for any necessary medications in case the medications become lost, and keep them separate from the medications themselves.

Preparation is the key when talking about staying healthy while traveling.

Consult the World Health Organization for International Travel

The World Health Organization lists a variety of travel-related health topics on its website at www.who.int/topics/en. As shown in Figure 8.5, this website has an alphabetical listing of health-related topics. It is very helpful in that you can look up any health problem you may have, such as asthma or diabetes, to get information about that disease and how it has affected people globally. The World Health Organization website also has specific information about disease outbreaks in all areas of the world. This includes full coverage of the avian influenza.

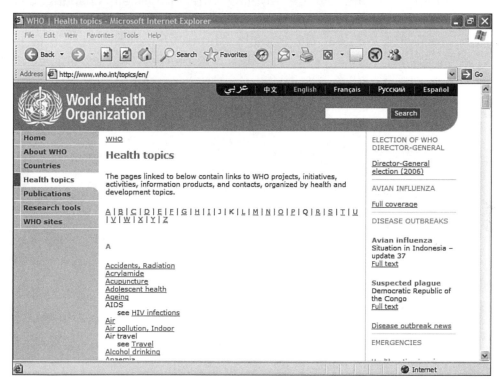

FIGURE 8.5
The World Health Organization website lists health topics alphabetically.

Supporting Travelers with Special Needs

Let's face it. No two travelers are alike. Everyone has his or her own unique needs. Technology and the Internet can help you arrange everything from wheelchairs to special meals for your distinctive travel needs.

Online Resources from the Access-Able Travel Source

If you or someone you are traveling with is physically challenged or has special needs, it is always good to check out the places you will visit for accessibility and special accommodations. One of the best Internet resources is the Access-Able Travel Source (www.access-able.com), shown in Figure 8.6.

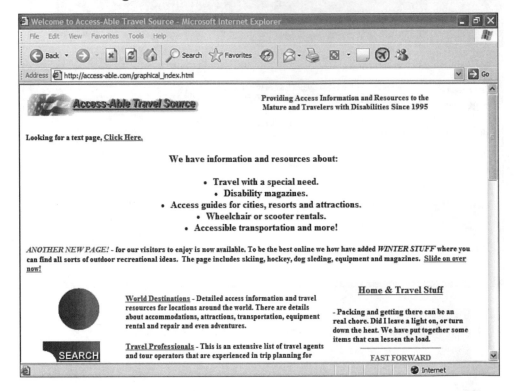

FIGURE 8.6
The Access-Able Travel Source website has detailed access information and travel resources for those with special needs.

This website was created by Bill Randall and his wife Carol, who has multiple sclerosis. They have done a great job of developing detailed access information for locations around the world. They offer many details about accommodations, attractions, equipment rental, and transportation. They also have honest assessments of cruise lines and airports. This website also contains two valuable lists. It has an extensive list of travel agents and tour operators who are experienced in trip planning for travelers with disabilities. It also links to more than 400 other websites in this area of expertise.

Online Resources from Frommer's

The Frommer's website also has valuable information for disabled travelers. Surf to www.frommers.com, click the Trip Ideas tab, and choose the Disabled menu item. Or you can access this Web area directly at www.frommers.com/trip_ideas/disabled.

As shown in Figure 8.7, at this site you find a link to a very useful and comprehensive article titled "Disabled Travelers: A Compendium of Trip Planning Resources." It lists agencies and operators who specialize in accessibility during travel. It also lists organizations that can help with your travel planning and execution.

Learning from others who are in the same position is always beneficial. The Frommer's discussion board for disabled travelers at http://www.frommers.com/cgi-bin/WebX?14@@.eead217 is a place where you can read about and learn from the experiences of others. You will find excellent information on these message boards. They discuss everything from tips on traveling with oxygen to traveling on dialysis to using an electric wheelchair in Europe.

Online Resources from the Seniors Travel Guide

Although many of today's hotels and resorts have accommodations for those with disabilities, it can be beneficial for the disabled traveler to check out those that cater to this clientele. The Seniors Travel Guide at http://seniorstravelguide.com, which is part of the Wired Seniors network, has a listing of accommodations and lodgings called disabilities resorts, as shown in Figure 8.8.

FIGURE 8.7
The Frommer's Disabled area has much comprehensive information in the article titled "Disabled Travelers: A Compendium of Trip Planning Resources."

Online Resources from Emerging Horizons' Accessible Travel

BLOOPER ALERT Foreign air carriers that fly to the U.S. do not have to adhere to the detailed disability laws that U.S. airlines must follow.

For more information on accessible travel, you may want to subscribe to the Emerging Horizons Accessible Travel magazine. It is geared toward people with mobility disabilities and includes everyone from slow walkers to wheelchair users. The Emerging Horizons website at http://emerging-horizons.com contains worthwhile sample articles and columns.

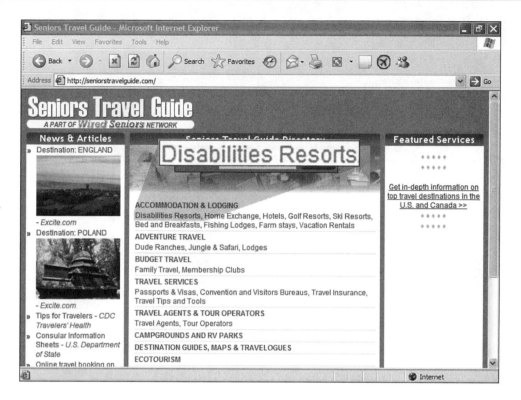

FIGURE 8.8
The Seniors Travel Guide lists disabilities resorts.

Other Online Resources for Travelers with Disabilities

You may also want to visit several other websites that specialize in assistive technology products and information on accessible travel. The ABLEDATA website provides information about assistive technology products for travelers in a special section at www.abledata.com. The link to this information is shown in Figure 8.9.

Some websites focus on just about every disability you can think of. Many of these sites have information on traveling with the many different types of disabilities. For instance, the Accessible Journeys website at www.disabilitytravel.com, shown in Figure 8.10, focuses on wheelchair travel. It has travel planning information and lists accessible group tours and cruises, special travel resources, and licensed travel companions.

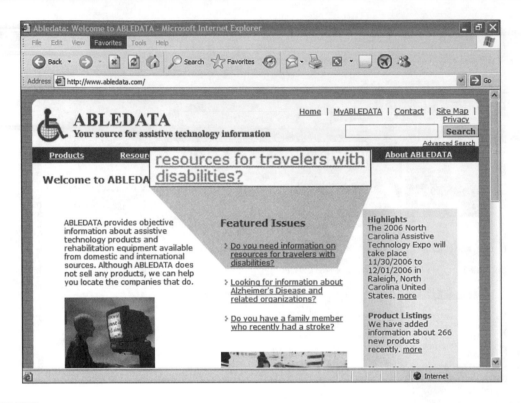

FIGURE 8.9
The ABLEDATA website has information and resources for travelers with disabilities.

BLOOPER ALERT

Some air carriers and other services require 48 hours advance notice for special accommodations that require preparation time.

The Trips Inc., Special Adventures website at www.tripsinc.com focuses on vacations for special travelers with developmental disabilities.

When dealing with disabilities, you can also use travel agents who specialize in making travel plans for people with physical disabilities. One such travel agency is Flying Wheels, which you can find at www.flyingwheelstravel.com.

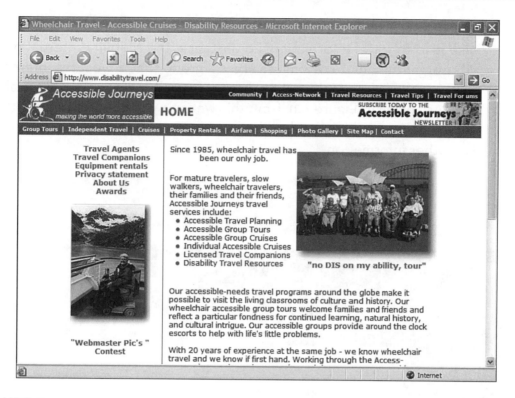

FIGURE 8.10
Wheelchair travel is the focus at the Accessible Journeys website.

Don't forget that you can often find information on traveling with disabilities by looking through the information for your destination. For instance, the All Go Here website at www.allgohere.com has an extensive directory of UK hotels and hospitality-related services that are disability-friendly. It also features an airline accessibility guide.

The Rotterdam accessibility guide at www.accessible.rotterdam.nl gives information on accessibility for all public buildings in Rotterdam.

Sandy's tip
To find information of this type, use a search engine such as Google at www.google.com. Type the name of your destination and the word "accessibility" in the search field.

Also be aware that websites that have information on disabilities can also lead to travel information. For instance, the Mobility International USA organization at www.miusa.org is a group that advocates international exchange and international development for people with disabilities. As shown in Figure 8.11, from this website you can search for other disability organizations and exchange programs, view new items, and see other information.

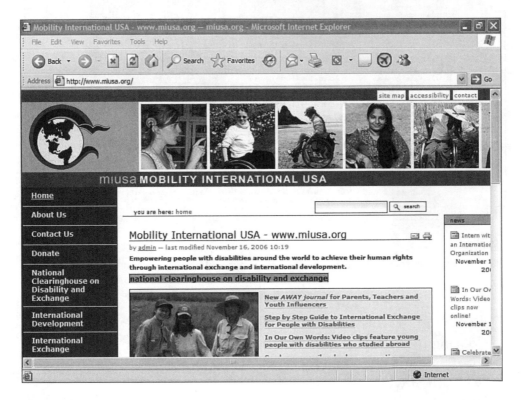

FIGURE 8.11
Mobility International USA is a great place to find out about exchange programs for people with disabilities.

As you know, air travel has changed dramatically since 9/11. Rules for travel can change at a moment's notice, so it is advisable for travelers with disabilities to check the current rules and regulations before they reach the airport. The Transportation Security Administration website has an area at www.tsa.gov/travelers/airtravel/specialneeds/index.shtm that has detailed information on screening procedures. You will also want to read its advice on how to declare and pack medications.

Traveling with Children

Preplanning is especially important when traveling with children. If you haven't traveled with kids since your own children were young, you may have to search your memory to recall all the things you did to help make the trip more enjoyable.

Remember that preparation is the key to traveling with children. Try to anticipate all the things that could go wrong and then take whatever you need to be prepared. Kids use a lot more Band-Aids than adults. Non-stinging anti-bacterial ointment is a must. And I always throw a few lollipops in a first aid kit for kids to help sweeten things up when cuts and bruises abound.

While you look for diversions and entertainment for the kids, don't forget that safe travel includes precautions that you take for safe travel with kids. The CDC has an excellent resource for traveling with children at www.cdc.gov/travel/child_travel.htm.

If you will be traveling by air, a lot has changed since you traveled with your own children. Be sure to check out the Transportation Security Administration's "Traveling with Children" bulletin at www.tsa.gov/travelers/airtravel/children/index.shtm. It gives information you need to know about the screening process, as well as travel tips and special information on children with disabilities.

Sandy's tip

If you will be taking children through airport screening, be sure to talk to them about the process in advance. It can be a little intimidating, even for some adults!

Another useful website for information on traveling with children is the AirSafe.com site at www.airsafe.com/kidsafe/kid_tips.htm, shown in Figure 8.12. Its "Top 10 Safety Tips for Traveling with Children" will help you in your quest to keep everyone safe and sound while having a great vacation.

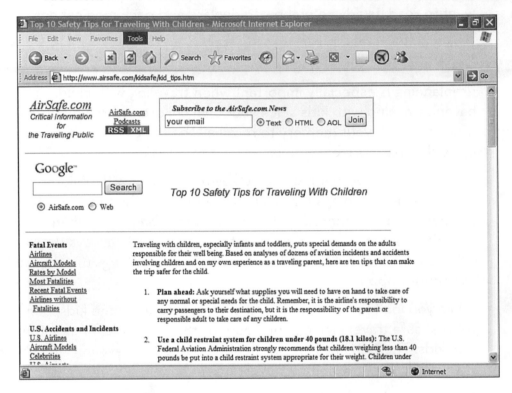

FIGURE 8.12
The AirSafe.com website has tips to make your trip with children safer and more fun.

Sandy's Summary

Even those with health problems are not ready to sit at home in a rocking chair. Nor should they have to. Today there are many resources for the traveler with special needs.

No matter what the status of your health, you will want to guard it on the road through proper preparation. Many online resources can help you prepare for a healthy and happy trip.

Internet resources also can help you with any special needs. From traveling in a wheelchair to obtaining special meals, these resources tell you what to expect and how to go about making the necessary arrangements.

Although traveling with children can be wonderful, they have special needs. Times have changed, and traveling with children is now quite different from when you took your own children along. Don't worry, though. Internet resources will help you get the kids organized and ready to hit the road.

Sandy Berger

Chapter 9

Traveling with Pets

I travel a lot; I hate having my life disrupted by routine.

—Caskie Stinnett

6 3% of U. S. households own a pet. That equates to pets in more than 69 million homes. We love our pets. We pamper them. It is estimated that we will spend more than $38 billion on our pets in 2007. That amount is poised to increase each year, as it has for the past twelve years.

More and more companies are realizing how beloved pets are and are creating products and services targeted directly at our pets. Many companies that previously focused only on humans are now turning their attention to our four-footed friends. Organizations such as Harley Davidson, Omaha Steaks, Origins, Old Navy, and Paul Mitchell offer lines of pet products, including pet shampoo, dog and cat attire, toys, and gourmet pet foods.

In This Chapter

- Finding Pet-Friendly Places
- Air Travel for Your Pet
- Motoring with Pets
- Camping with Pets
- RVing with Pets
- Pet Health on the Road
- Pet Safety and Security

Hotel chains across the country are welcoming pets. So, if you just can't bear to leave Rover or Kitty at the kennel, no problem. You can bring them along. The Internet will help you find places to stay. Did you know that even some beaches welcome dogs?

Finding Pet-Friendly Places

When you travel with a pet, you don't want to go from hotel to hotel to find one that takes pets—and you don't have to. Just use your computer and Web browser to find a great place to stay.

When choosing a place to vacation with your pet, you have a wide variety of choices. Many people think that large cities are not pet-friendly, but information from the DogFriendly.com website shatters that myth. New York has 30 off-leash dog parks and areas scattered throughout the city. Los Angeles County has a three-acre "Dog Beach Zone" for off-leash dogs. St. Louis is home to a dog-friendly AKC Museum of the Dog. DogFriendly.com lists the Top 10 Cities to Visit in the United States and Canada:

- Vancouver, British Columbia
- San Francisco
- Chicago
- Boston
- Austin, Texas
- Seattle
- New York City
- Long Beach (Los Angeles area)
- St Louis
- Northern Virginia (Washington, D.C. area)

More information on each city is given at the website, making www. DogFriendly.com a great place to find a pet-friendly vacation spot.

Restaurants and Lodging

A good area to start your online search is the Pets Welcome website at www.petswelcome.com. As shown in Figure 9.1, it has a comprehensive state-by-state list of pet-friendly hotels in the U. S. and Canada. I have visited this website for years, and it just keeps getting better and better. It now lists more than 25,000 hotels, ski resorts, campgrounds, and beaches that welcome animals. It even has listings of bed-and-breakfast lodgings that accept pets.

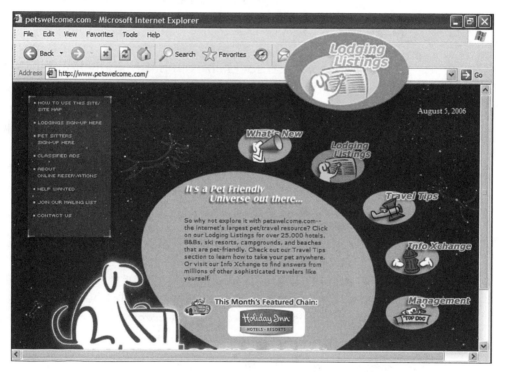

FIGURE 9.1
Pets Welcome is a website with an abundance of both good humor and pet information.

You'll find that www.petswelcome.com has a permeating sense of humor and love of animals. They list Smudge Kingsley, a Bracco Italiano bird dog, as CEO of their company. Lola, a Gordon setter, is the CFO, and Jill, a hard-working cat, is the "glue that keeps the whole petswelcome.com organization together." Although all this may sound a bit

Sandy's tip

The ownership of hotels can change hands often. Always call or email the hotel before you leave to make sure that their pet-friendly attitude hasn't changed.

BLOOPER ALERT

Some hotels have a one-pet limit. If you are traveling with two or more pets, check this out when you make your reservations.

hokey, it does make for an interesting website, and the information at Petswelcome just can't be beat!

Another good website for finding pet-friendly hotels is Travel Pets at www.travelpets.com. Travel Pets has a worldwide lodging list, a free newsletter, and even a travel checklist for your pet.

1Click Pet Hotels at www.1clickpethotels.com is another good resource for finding hotels that both you and your pet can enjoy.

The Pets on the Go website at www.petsonthego. com also specializes in pet-friendly hotel listings. The website isn't pretty, and the interface could be easier to use. For instance, states, provinces, and countries are listed together alphabetically, and cities are listed right next to them. In some cases, you have to dig for the information. Yet this site is still a useful place to visit for finding a place to stay with your pet.

For an extensive listing of pet-friendly hotels, visit www.takeyourpet.com. This site also lists thousands of veterinarians, animal hospitals, shelters, groomers, and kennels and boarding facilities. They even list sitting services and pet supply stores all over the United States. The takeyourpet.com website also has a free pet travel newsletter and travel tips and guides.

Like many other websites, Pet Friendly Travel at www.petfriendly-travel.com has listings of pet-friendly hotels, dog parks, and dog beaches. It also has one unique feature: reviews of pet-friendly restaurants and bars from around the country. You can read other people's reviews or add your own, giving each restaurant a rating from one to three bones.

As a dog lover, another of my favorite "rovin' with Rover" websites is DogFriendly.com (www.DogFriendly.com). You can find dog-friendly hotels by selecting a state in the Travel Guides for Dogs area, as shown in Figure 9.2. Besides hotels and accommodations, the DogFriendly.com website also has comprehensive lists of RV parks and campgrounds, beaches, parks, hiking trails, and off-leash dog parks. It also has an outdoor dining guide and dog-friendly attractions and events. You will find much valuable information on the DogFriendly.com website. You can even sign up for its free newsletter.

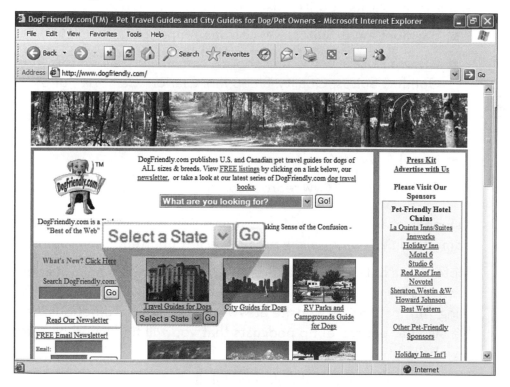

FIGURE 9.2
The Travel Guides for Dogs area at DogFriendly.com.

Many hotel chains welcome pets, but some chains are not owned by a single parent company. Instead, they are franchised, and every individual hotel may have many different owners. Even those hotel chains owned by a single parent company may be run by different management companies. While most owners and managers follow the ground rules set by the parent company, they are often allowed to set their own policies. Also, local regulations regarding pets can vary from one location to the next, and hotels must follow these local laws.

So although I will give you a list of hotel chains that welcome pets, you should always check with each individual hotel to confirm its pet policy.

Here is a list of a few of the more popular hotels that let you bring along your four-legged friends:

- Baymont Inn & Suites: www.baymontinns.com
- Choice Hotels: www.choicehotels.com. Includes Comfort Inn, Comfort Suites, Quality, Sleep Inn, Clarion, Cambria Suites, MainStay Suites, Suburban, EconoLodge, and Rodeway Inns.
- Holiday Inn and Holiday Inn Express: www.ichotelsgroup.com
- Motel 6: www.Motel6.com
- Red Roof Inns: www.redroof.com/promotions/pets.asp

Ask beforehand if you can leave your pet in the room unattended. Some facilities do not allow pets to be left unattended in rooms.

Motel 6 is a hotel chain that accepts pets in most of their locations. It even has animal expert Jack Hanna write special articles regarding traveling with pets on its website at www.motel6.com/promotions/pets.asp. He also has pet travel tip podcasts that you will find listed on the Motel 6 website.

Motel 6 spells out its pet policy in detail on its website. Its policy is similar to many other hotel and motel chains:

- One well-behaved pet per room is permitted unless prohibited by state law or ordinance. Service animals are always allowed.
- Pets must be declared at check-in.
- Pets should never be left alone in a room or automobile.
- If a pet is left unattended in the room, we will not clean due to safety concerns for our employees and the pet. Guests may be

asked to vacate the property if their pet becomes a nuisance to other guests.

- Pets must be on a leash or properly carried outside guest rooms.

- When walking pets on the property, please be considerate of other guests and clean up after your pet.

Although Motel 6 allows you to leave your pet unattended in the room, other hotels like Red Roof Inns do not. Always ask what the "in-room-alone" pet policy is.

While many hotels simply accept pets, some have unleashed a more-than-friendly welcome. If you want to treat your pet like royalty, check out some of the pampered-pet packages that are available at high-end hotels. For instance, the W Hotels have a pampered-pet program that can be found at www.starwoodhotels.com/promotions/promo_landing.html?category=WPETS.

BLOOPER ALERT
Hotel information can change quickly, and websites are not always up-to-date. Be sure to contact the hotel to confirm that it allows pets and to clarify its pet rules and surcharges.

BLOOPER ALERT
Watch your pets in hotel lobbies and outdoor areas. Fountains in hotels and public locations sometimes contain antifreeze, which is poisonous to pets.

At participating W Hotels, your pet can have his or her own custom W pet bed, a toy and treat at check-in, and a special treat at turndown. Concierge services include dog sitting, dog walking, and grooming services. In fact, if you stay at the W, your pet can even get a special birthday cake.

The Loews Hotels Pampered Pets packages (www.loewshotels.com/packages.asp?type=pets) include a room service meal for your pet.

Your four-legged friends are sure to approve of these pampered-pet hotels.

Parks and Recreation

Sometimes when traveling, it is good to be able to let your four-legged friends run loose and stretch their legs. And what dog owner wouldn't be enticed by an afternoon of playing with his or her pet in a beautiful park? The Dogpark.com website at www.dogpark.com, as shown in Figure 9.3, helps you find dog parks in the U.S. and Canada.

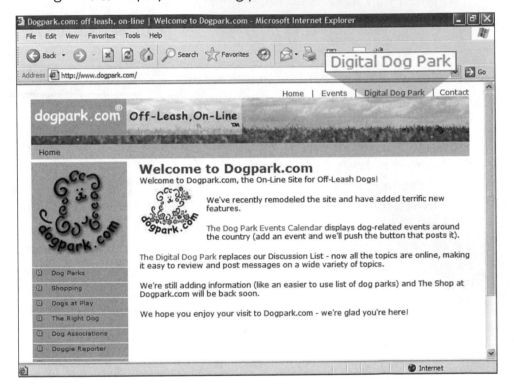

FIGURE 9.3
The Digital Dog Park at www.dogpark.com includes information on dog parks and doggie events.

Dog Beaches and Campsites

On a recent trip to Florida, I was amazed at the number of dog beaches. The Florida is Kind to Canines website at www.doortosummer. com/door/civic/beachptsfrm.htm has a comprehensive list of Florida beaches that allow dogs.

Florida is not the only state that welcomes dogs at some of its beaches. The BeachCalifornia.com website at www.beachcalifornia.com tells you everything you want to know about California beaches. Its pet area at www.beachcalifornia.com/california-dog-beaches.html, shown in Figure 9.4, has an extensive list of California dog beaches and pet-friendly parks.

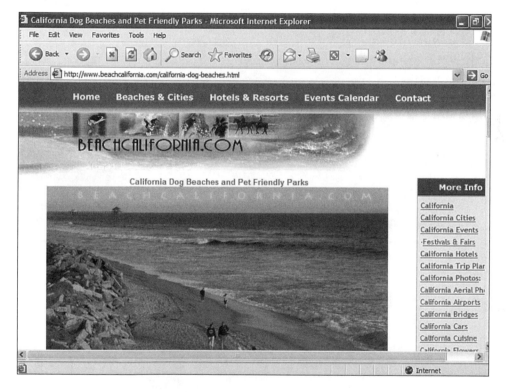

FIGURE 9.4
The pet area at BeachCalifornia.com.

At www.beachcalifornia.com/california-dog-beaches.html you can find a good listing of dog beaches in California.

Here are some other websites that list dog beaches and camping areas:

- Pets Welcome at www.petswelcome.com

- Pet Friendly Travel at www.petfriendlytravel.com

- DogFriendly.com at www.DogFriendly.com

For more ideas on pet-friendly vacations, you may want to consider joining a pet travel club like Take Your Pet (www.takeyourpet.com). For $14.95 a year the site offers a directory of more than 40,000 properties and lists animal hospitals, shelters, and other pet-related resources. The club offers discounts and bulletin boards. A $1.95 five-day trial is available.

If you don't find the vacation you would like, you can create your own. The website Rovin' With Rover (www.rovinwithrover.com) shows you how to create tours for you and your pets (see Figure 9.5).

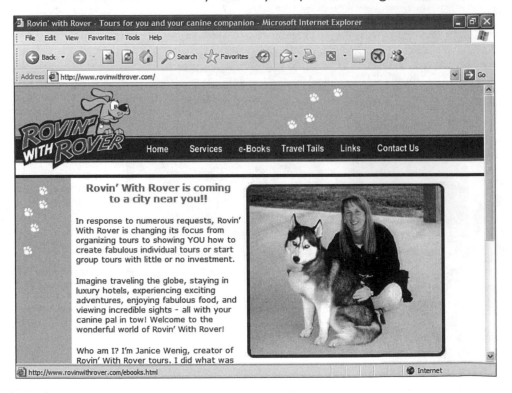

FIGURE 9.5
The Rovin' With Rover website show you how to create canine travel tours.

Air Travel for Your Pet

According to the Department of Transportation, more than "two million pets and live animals are transported by air every year in the United States."

When you decide to take your pet along on that airplane, you must consider many things. The airlines state unequivocally that animals can safely be transported in their planes, but some animal-rights groups have a differing opinion. They pressed for the Department of Transportation regulation that was passed in May 2005 requiring all airlines to file monthly reports of incidents involving the loss, injury, or death of animals during air transport.

sandy's tip
The American Veterinary Medical Association recommends against tranquilizing pets before air travel. Breathing problems and other side effects can be more dangerous than having the pet become agitated.

These reports are made public, but they can be difficult to find. If you are interested in knowing how many pets are lost or injured or die during air transport, you will want to visit ThirdAmendment.com at www.thirdamendment.com/animals.html. This website has links to the data on the reports, which may help you choose which airline you will use. For instance, the yearly report from May 2005 to May 2006 listed Continental Airlines as reporting eight deaths and eight injuries. US Airways had only one death and one injury. That statistic alone may help you decide which airline to use.

The Pet Professor also has a comprehensive list of pet-friendly airlines at www.thepetprofessor.com/articles/article.aspx?id=240, as shown in Figure 9.6.

BLOOPER ALERT
With some airlines, liability differs for pets checked as baggage versus those traveling as air cargo. Always check with your airline about their liability and the best way to check in your pet.

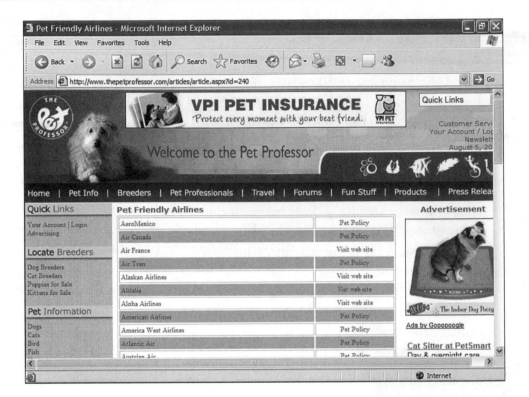

FIGURE 9.6
The Pet Professor website has links to pet information from many different airlines.

The Pet Professor's links take you directly to each airline and/or to its posted pet policy. This means that the information you get there should be up-to-date. However, you should always check directly with the airline you will use about its rules and regulations regarding transporting your pet. Each airline establishes its own policy and rules for transporting animals, and these rules can change at any time.

The Internet is a good place to find tips on air travel with your pets. The Pet Friendly Travel Pet Air Travel area at www.petfriendlytravel. com/?page=airtravel is filled with safe travel tips. The Humane Society of the United States at www.hsus.org/pets/pet_care/caring_for_pets_ when_you_travel/traveling_by_air_with_pets/ has a myriad of tips for air travel with pets, as shown in Figure 9.7.

FIGURE 9.7
The Humane Society has tips for safe air travel for your pets.

You can also access safety tips for pet travel at most airline websites and at http://airlines.ws, a comprehensive directory of the world's airlines, airline news, polls, and commentary.

Pets as Carry-On Baggage

Recently some airlines started allowing small pets to ride in a cargo bag under the passenger's seat. The Federal Aviation Administration (FAA) allows each airline to decide if it will let you travel with your pet in the passenger cabin and to impose its own restrictions, so you must check with your airline for its rules and regulations. If the airline you use allows your pet in the cabin, it considers the pet container to be carry-on baggage. Therefore, it must follow the rules for carry-ons, which can be found at the Federal Aviation Administration website at http://faa.gov.

These rules include the following:

■ The pet container must fit under the seat without blocking any-one's access to the plane's main aisle.

■ The pet container must be stowed properly before the plane's last passenger entry door is closed and the plane leaves the gate.

■ The pet container must remain properly stowed the entire time the airplane is moving on the tarmac and during takeoff and landing.

■ You must follow flight attendant instructions regarding the proper stowage of your pet con-tainer.

Sandy's tip
Most airlines limit the number of pets that can be in the cabin, so if you want to bring your pet onboard with you, it's good to make reservations early.

More information on bringing your pets into the cabin can be found at the Department of Transportation (http://airconsumer.ost.dot.gov/publications/animals.htm) and the U.S. Department of Agriculture (www.aphis.usda.gov).

Other Requirements

Although regulations vary, just about every airline requires a health cer-tificate for the pet and charges an additional fee for its travel. Most air-lines also require a special animal container and have a list of pets that can be transported. Some have weather-related restrictions, in which they refuse to transport pets during extremely hot or cold weather.

BLOOPER ALERT
Animal health certificates have expiration dates. Make sure your animal's certificate will cover your travel dates.

Although the airlines have many rules about trans-porting pets, they are not necessarily as anti-pet as you might imagine. Some airlines even cater to pets. Israel's El Al Airlines has a pet frequent-flyer program called the Points for Pets Program. Virgin Atlantic offers pets free gifts, including collar tags for dogs and a Virgin scarf for ferrets.

Even though many airlines welcome pets, some countries do not. Many different areas of the world require special vaccinations and/or quarantines. The state of Hawaii has pet quarantines to prevent the spread of rabies. So be sure to check your travel destination for its rules and regulations. Unless you plan an extended stay in a country with a lengthy quarantine, you may want to leave your pet at home when traveling to certain areas.

> *sandy's tip*
> When you travel, especially by air, a big bag of dog food can be cumbersome. It may be easier to order the dog food online before your trip and have it delivered to your hotel.

In cases like this, you may want to consider boarding your pet, finding a friend or neighbor to keep him, or hiring a pet sitter.

Pet quarantines are being shortened or eliminated in certain cases, so be sure you check out the country you are visiting. Also, some airlines may be approved to bring pets into certain countries, and others may not be. For instance, cats and dogs traveling to London can avoid the usual six-month quarantine by flying Continental Airlines, which has been approved under the United Kingdom's "Pet Travel Scheme."

> **BLOOPER ALERT**
> Before you travel somewhere, be sure there are no pet restrictions where you're going. Most countries impose strict pet quarantines of several months, so unless you plan an extended stay, international pet travel is unrealistic in some cases.

If you are traveling internationally, you can find more extensive information at the International Air Transport Association (IATA) website at www.iata.org. IATA is a global trade organization with plenty of information on traveling with your dog or cat.

Sandy's tip

Besides a crate of the appropriate size, many airlines also require that the pet have absorbent material to lie on in the crate. Check on this requirement before you leave home.

The laws regarding the types of shots an animal is required to have vary from state to state. A trip to the state's website may be in order before you leave. Although an animal may be able to disembark without the required shots, he may not be able to fly out of the state. That can be a real bummer when you travel. So be sure to check before you leave, unless you want an extended vacation while you find a vet to administer the proper vaccinations.

Motoring with Pets

Everyone knows that traveling by car or motor home with a pet can be trying for everyone involved. Good preparation can make the difference between a difficult trip and an enjoyable one. Renowned animal expert Jack Hanna has teamed with Motel 6 to offer tips on traveling with pets. Among his tips for car travel with pets are the following:

- Use a pet travel crate.
- If your pet isn't in a crate, use a pet restraining device.
- Put local contact information on your pet's collar tag.
- Give animals plenty of water or ice.
- Identify pet-friendly hotels and motels.
- Never leave children or animals unattended in a vehicle.

Hanna also recommends pet-safe ventilation grills for car windows. A pet that has enough room to stick its head out the window often can maneuver its entire body through that partially open window. Also, road debris could possibly hit your dog in the eye. More tips as well as a podcast of pet travel tips are available at the Motel 6 website at www.motel6.com/promotions/pets_june.asp.

More car travel tips can be found at the Paws Across America website at www.pawsacrossamerica.com/car.html. Following some of the simple tips listed at these websites can help you make sure your car doesn't become a zoo during your road trip.

Camping with Pets

Camping with your pet can be an exciting experience, but remember that your pet is not used to the "wild," so you should do a little planning to make sure the trip goes smoothly. Some basic preparation can ensure your pet's safety and enhance his enjoyment as well as your own.

The RVtravel.com website lists Ten Commandments for Camping with Dogs at http://rvtravel.com/publish/article_697.shtml:

1   Make sure your dog can't get lost.

2   Get all his vaccinations up to date.

3   Make your dog easy to identify.

4   Clean up after your dog.

5   Learn how to provide first aid to your dog.

6   Involve your dog in everything you do.

7   Call the campgrounds before you go.

8   Plan ahead for the unexpected.

9   Learn about your camping environment.

10 Recognize and respect the views of others.

More details are available at the website. Of course, many of these suggestions also pertain to cats, ferrets, and other pets.

The Internet is filled with tips on keeping your pets happy and healthy while camping. The National Park Service at www.nps.gov/pub_aff/e-mail/pets.htm gives all the rules and restrictions for pets who visit these parks. It also has information on the possibility of pets encountering wild animals.

If you are looking for a place to camp with your pet, the PetFriendly Travel website has an area called Pets in National Parks & National Forests. You can find this area at www.petfriendlytravel.com/?page=national_parks. It lists national parks that you can enjoy with your pets.

The Hike with your Dog website at www.hikewithyourdog.com has links to more than 2,000 dog-friendly parks and trails in the United States and Canada. This site also lists parks that do not allow dogs, making it a good place to check before you complete your hiking and camping plans.

RVing with Pets

Most of the travel tips that apply to pets traveling in cars also apply to RV travel. Yet traveling with your pets in an RV can pose additional concerns.

Sandy's tip

Most car and RV rental companies allow the use of their vehicles to transport pets, but it is good to call first and ask about their pet policy. Some charge a pet deposit fee to cover possible damage.

Most pets love to travel with their owners, and their presence on a road trip can mean comfort and companionship for both owners and their animal friends. Because RV travel is often of longer duration than a simple overnight to the campground, preparing for your pet's travel is very important.

For information on RVing with your pets, surf to the RVtravel.com website at http://rvtravel.com/publish/cat_index_78.shtml. You will find articles on security for your pets on the go, information on feeding your pet on the road, and a list of pet supplies you shouldn't be without when traveling.

Although the RVing With Dogs website at www.rvingwithdogs.com focuses on doggy information, much of its information can be applied to other pets as well. It lists 135 campsites across the country. It also has information on packing for your pooch and even has recipes for doggy nourishment on the road.

Pet Health on the Road

If a person gets sick on the road, emergency help is always available. But that's not true for our four-footed friends. So it's very important that we guard their health when on the road.

Before setting out, check with your veterinarian to make sure that all your pet's vaccinations are up to date. If your pet is overdue for a medical assessment, be sure to do that before you leave. While at the vet's office, you can get your pet's medical records. Make two copies—one to keep in a safe place at home and one to take on the road with you.

Make sure that the records include your pet's current rabies certificate. It is required in all 50 states and may come in handy for entry to certain areas or if a sticky situation arises.

Also prepare for travel with your pet by making sure that you have effective flea and tick medication on hand, as well as any other medication that your pet may need.

Because it is not always easy to find medical help for your pet on the road, you may want to keep available a list of veterinary hospitals. If you travel with a laptop, you can use it to search for a hospital if the need arises. If you don't take a laptop with you, search online before you leave, and make a list of locations and contact information for animal hospitals in the areas you will visit.

BLOOPER ALERT
Your pet encounters a lot of changes to his environment when you travel. Don't change his food suddenly. Make sure his regular food is available when you are on the road.

A great online resource for emergency help for your pets is Healthlypet's Hospital Locator at www.healthypet.com. As shown in Figure 9.8, this website lists American Animal Hospital Association-accredited pet hospitals throughout the United States and Canada. It also has an impressive core of articles on canine vaccine guidelines, parasite protection, and a complete pet care library that includes information on cats, dogs, hedgehogs, rabbits, ferrets, and other animal friends.

FIGURE 9.8
The Healthypet.com website helps you find emergency medical aid for your pet anywhere in the United States.

Pet First Aid Kit

You always need to be prepared for circumstances when your pet may need medical treatment. Certainly the first aid kit you create for yourself can also be used for your pets, but some additional items may be needed. Be sure to include tweezers, pliers, and a magnifying glass.

Remember to include everything you may need for an injury, sickness, bite, or inflammation. The Animal Referral and Emergency Center of Arizona suggests that your pet first aid kit include bandage rolls, bandage tape, scissors, large square gauze pads, terrycloth towels, tweezers, pliers, magnifying glass, triple-antibiotic ointment, disposable iodine wipes, hydrogen peroxide, rubbing alcohol, milk of magnesia, thermometer, pet shampoo, leash, soft, adjustable muzzle, latex gloves, and blankets.

It is a good idea to keep these items in a waterproof container marked with your name, address, and phone numbers. If you will be creating one kit for both humans and pets, include the names and numbers of your doctors and veterinarians as well as poison control hotlines. Include your medical records and those of your pet. Make sure your pet's information includes name, age, breed, sex, and any identification information such as microchipping.

It is also advisable to have an emergency procedure handbook available. If you don't have one, you can print emergency procedures from the DoctorDog.com website. The Dog Owner's Home Veterinary Handbook information is at www.doctordog.com/dogbook/dogch01.html. The Cat Owner's Book is at www.doctordog.com/catbook/catch01.html.

The Partnership for Animal Welfare (PAW) website at www.paw-rescue.org has excellent emergency medical information as well as a list of recommended items for your pet's first aid kit, as shown in Figure 9.9. The emergency treatment and kit instructions for dogs are at www.paw-rescue.org/PAW/PETTIPS/DogTip_FirstAid.php.

When developing your first aid kit, be sure to consider the time of year during which you will be traveling, because needs for cold weather may differ from those for the hot summer months. Also take into consideration special events that you may be attending or everyday events that could impact your pet. For instance, if you are traveling on the 4th of July with an easily agitated pet, you may want to consider some tranquilizers or other calming equipment for when the fireworks start.

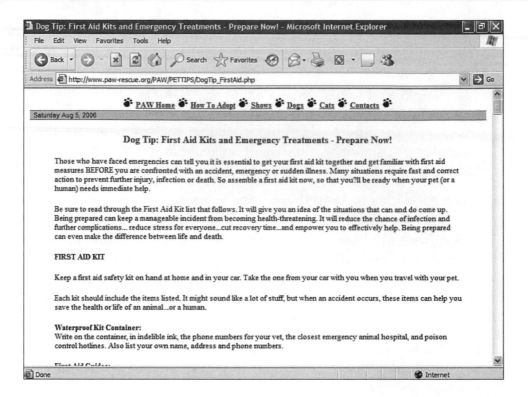

FIGURE 9.9
The PAW website lists suggested items for a pet first aid kit.

Pet Safety and Security

When you are on the road, remember to take your pet's safety and security as seriously as that for the rest of the family. Experts recommend travel crates and pens for your pet's safety on the road.

One of the biggest threats to a traveling pet is that he has a better chance of being separated from his owner while traveling. According to the National Humane Society and the National Council of Pet Population Study and Policy, more than ten million pets become lost each year. Only one in ten is found. If your pet is lost in his home environment, he may return on his own, or you may find him. When you travel, both you and your pet are in unfamiliar territory, making the return of a lost pet even more difficult.

However, you can take steps to keep your pet secure while ensuring a safe return if he is lost.

A watchful eye, crates, leashes, and other security equipment are essential. Large portable exercise pens are also available to let your pets have some freedom while being securely enclosed.

sandy's tip
Always have a picture of your pet with you when you travel in case he gets lost or stolen.

Remember to have identification on your pet and to carry a photo of your pet so that he can be easily identified if lost.

If you are an RVer or you and your pet travel often, you might want to consider having your pet microchipped. This is a painless procedure that permanently identifies your pet and can be used to return him if he is lost.

The two main microchip companies in the United States are AVID FriendChip (www.avidmicrochip.com) and HomeAgain Microchip Identification System (www. homeagainid.com). More information on these companies can be found on their websites. An actual chip used is pictured on the AVID MicroChip I.D. website, as shown in Figure 9.10.

LINGO

A *microchip* is a very small sterile transponder that is inserted under the pet's skin. It contains a unique ID code that can be read by a scanner to identify your pet.

The chip gives your pet a unique identification number. That ID number is listed in a database with information about your pet as well as your contact information. If your address and/or telephone numbers change, you can easily change that information in the database.

Animal shelters, animal control officers, and veterinarians across the country have universal scanners that can read the information on the chip from either company. They simply call an 800 number with the pet's ID and are given the information necessary to reunite the pet with his or her owner.

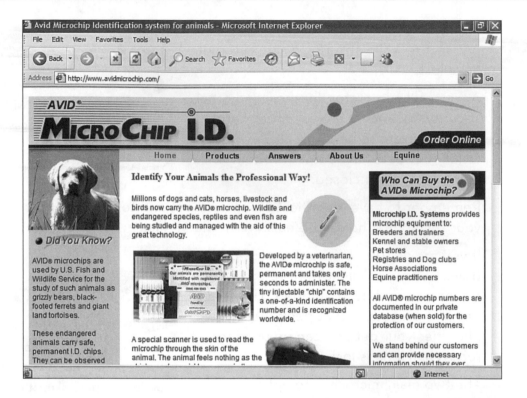

FIGURE 9.10
The AVID MicroChip I.D. website shows what a microchip looks like.

Sandy's tip
When camping or RVing with a pet, it's a good idea to put your license plate number and cell phone number on the pet's tag to make returning a lost pet who's away from home easier.

When the microchip is implanted, your pet is given an ID tag indicating that he has been microchipped. All animal shelters and humane societies routinely scan animals they receive. So there is a good chance that if your microchipped pet is lost, he will be returned even if he is not wearing his ID tag.

Microchipping is not just for cats and dogs. The U.S. Fish and Wildlife Service microchips grizzly bears, black-footed ferrets, and giant land tortoises. Even birds, llamas, pigs, rabbits, snakes, and lizards can be microchipped.

Sandy's Summary

Traveling with Rover, Kitty, or your other animals can be fun. They are part of the family, so why not bring them along? The Internet makes it easy to find pet-friendly hotels and motels. It even helps you find beaches, restaurants, and events that welcome you and your animals.

Air travel places special restrictions on your pets, but if you know about them ahead of time, you can still travel quite easily with your pet. Internet resources will help you find the best airline to use, as well as help you prepare for your trip so that it is as uneventful as possible.

Motoring with your pets can be fun as long as you make the right preparations, such as knowing where to get help for your pet at your destination and creating a pet-specific first aid kit. My tips and the Internet will tell you everything you need to know.

If you and your pet love to camp, the Internet will help you find a good place to visit and give you important information that will make your expedition more enjoyable.

Remember that you are responsible for your pet's safety and security when you are on the road. Having the proper supplies, identification, and emergency equipment can save you hours of anxiety and frustration. Microchipping provides an extra level of security to ensure your pet's safe return should you become separated.

Your pet may be your best friend, but when you want to take him on the road, Internet resources are another friendly companion.

Sandy Berger

Chapter 10

Stay Online on the Go

A good traveler has no fixed plans, and is not intent on arriving.

—Lao Tzu

These days it easy to stay connected as long as you make the right preparations. You can leave your computer at home and use Internet cafés, libraries, and hotels to communicate seamlessly on the go. Or you can bring your laptop and seek out hotspots. This chapter gives you tips and tricks for staying online when you are on the road.

IN THIS CHAPTER

- Getting Online Without a Laptop
- Using Your Laptop on the Road
- Traveling with Your Laptop
- Safe Surfing
- Online Overseas

LINGO

A *hotspot* is a high-speed wireless Internet access point that is provided in public locations.

Getting Online Without a Laptop

Using a computer and the Internet on a daily basis has become a way of life for many of us. Internet resources can be valuable when you are traveling, and email is a great way to stay in touch. Luckily, whether you travel with a laptop computer or you prefer to leave your computer at home, you can still hook up to the Internet when you are on the road.

Finding Access to the Internet as You Travel

LINGO

Broadband is a high-speed Internet connection—generally using a cable connection or a special telephone line (DSL)—that makes Internet pages appear and files download more quickly. A broadband connection is always on, so your computer doesn't have to dial to initiate the connection. Technically speaking, broadband communication speeds typically start at 384 kilobytes per second. Broadband is typically 10 to 20 times faster than the traditional dial-up modem.

Don't have a laptop? Or don't want to lug it around? No problem. There are many places that you can get access to the Internet without having a computer.

Hotels

If you are staying at a hotel, that should be the first place you look for Internet access. Five years ago it was hard to find a hotel with Internet access, but times have changed. Now most hotels have some method of helping you get on the Web.

Many hotels have broadband Internet access for their guests who bring along laptops, and some also provide computers for their guests to use.

Some hotel chains are becoming noted for their free Internet service. Hilton's Hampton Inn and Hampton Inn Suites offer free Internet access in all rooms and free wireless in lobbies. Many Marriott Courtyard and Residence Inns have free Internet service in the rooms. Most AmeriSuites have Internet access in the rooms as well as the lobby.

Some hotel chains like Best Western offer free wired or Wi-Fi Internet service in a percentage of the hotel's rooms, so it is always good to request Internet service when you make your hotel reservations.

Many higher-end hotels have business centers supplied with Internet-connected computers, printers, and fax machines. Some are free, some charge an hourly fee, and some charge a daily fee for use.

Some hotels have computers set up in the lobby for guests to use. I have seen this in several cities in Europe as well as here in the States. In almost all cases, these hotels let me use their lobby computers even if I was not a hotel guest, as long as they were available and no registered guests were waiting to use them.

> *sandy's tip*
> Always check with your hotel before you set out on your trip to see whether it provides Internet access in the rooms and/or lobby and whether it has computers available for guests to use.

Some hotels also offer Internet connections through the television. Just follow the instruction card, and you can access the Internet right on the television in your room.

If you are in a really high-end hotel, you may even find the Internet available through a mirror on the wall. Believe it or not, Philips has created mirrors that turn into Internet monitors. It is selling this product to hotels and motels around the world.

Be sure to ask about the hotel's Internet connectivity and the availability of computers that have Internet access when you make your reservation.

Public Libraries

If you are traveling by RV or your hotel doesn't have a computer available for your use, public libraries are a good option. Some libraries have computers with Internet connectivity that are free for visitors. Because this service is quite popular, some libraries impose time limits on computer use.

College Campuses

Another place to find a free Internet-connected computer is on colleges campuses. Some colleges and universities have computers scattered around the campus that are free for students and visitors to use.

Cybercafes

Cybercafes have computers with Internet access available for public use. Most are also equipped with printers. There is generally a charge for using these computers, and rates vary greatly. Sometimes if the cybercafe is an eating establishment, you can get free use of its computer with a food purchase.

Cafés of this type can be found all over the world. They are especially plentiful and relatively cheap in rural areas that are popular with backpackers. Sometimes cybercafes also have connections available where you can hook up your laptop computer, but it's usually easier to use the equipment they provide.

For a listing of cybercafes all over the world, check out Cybercafes at www.cybercafe.com. As shown in Figure 10.1, you simply click the area you are interested in on the map. Cybercafes has a database of more than 4,000 Internet cafés in 140 different countries.

Another website called The Cybercafe Search Engine at www.cybercaptive.com performs much the same function. It lists more than 5,000 cybercafes in 161 countries. Although the interface is a bit confusing and the flashing ad at the top of the page is distracting, this website can be a useful resource when you are looking for a cybercafe.

Office Supply Stores

Not every community has a cybercafe. If you need a computer while traveling in the States and you can't find a library or cybercafes, try the local office supply store. Many now offer computers for public use. Most FedEx Kinko's stores have complete workstations available for use. You pay for the service, but the convenience may be worth it since many of their stores are open 24/7. You can get a list of FedEx Kinko's stores for any area at www.kinkos.com.

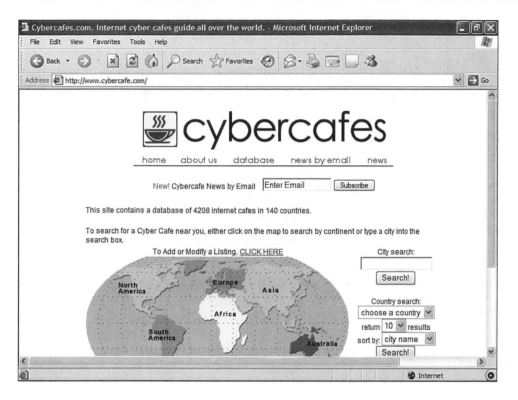

FIGURE 10.1
The Cybercafes website helps you find computers to use in 140 different countries.

Taking Your Data on the Road

When traveling without a computer, you can use a USB flash drive to carry all your documents and data. These are very small portable devices that plug in the USB port on a computer. They are a boon to the traveler who doesn't want to lug a computer around. These devices can carry all your files for use at any computer you happen upon during your travels. They can be kept in your purse or pocket, worn around your neck, or attached to your keychain.

LINGO

USB flash drives are also called "pen drives," "keychain drives," "key drives," "USB keys," "USB sticks," and "memory keys."

LINGO

To **sync** means to synchronize the data so that the files in both places are updated with the most current versions.

Some recently developed software makes a USB flash drive even more useful for travelers. Your USB drive can be easily loaded with special software that lets you take most of your files with you quite easily. The top two software programs of this type are Migo (www.migosoftware.com) and U3 (www.u3.com).

This type of software is installed to the USB drive. Before you leave home, you insert the USB drive into your computer and sync all your data. Then, when you are at any computer, you simply plug the USB drive into the computer you are using, and you can access all your data. All your data is encrypted and password-protected. All of it runs right from the USB drive, so no trace of your personal information is left on the computer you just visited.

BLOOPER ALERT

If you use a public computer to check your email, be sure to log out properly so that the next person will not have access to your email.

This type of software is fairly new, but it is already very useful. Both Migo and U3 are developing quickly and are adding new features on a regular basis. Both programs are inexpensive and can be purchased on a USB flash drive or downloaded separately for use on a drive you already own. I find that Migo is currently easier to use, but you may want to investigate both.

Using Your Laptop on the Road

If you travel with a portable computer, you now have a myriad of options for Internet access that have become available in the last few years. You can surf the Internet in parks, hotels, restaurants, and other establishments around the world.

Finding a Hotspot

New hotspots are proliferating quickly across the country. Parks, airports, restaurants, coffee shops, convenience stores, and truck stops are now Internet hotspots. At many places the access is free, but at some you have to pay a fee for the access.

Many major cities have free wireless service in their major parks. On a recent trip to New York, I surfed the Internet on my laptop from a bench in Battery Park. I also surfed the Web at New York's City Hall. Some cities like San Jose and San Francisco are setting up wireless networks to blanket the entire city.

You can't see the wireless waves traveling through the air, so it is possible to be in a wireless hotspot and not know it if you don't have a hotspot finder or laptop with you.

Hotspots have become widespread, but finding one to hook up to can be a chore. Fortunately, technology and the Internet will come to your aid.

Electronic Hotspot Finders

If you travel a lot, you can make the task of finding a hotspot much easier by purchasing a small device called a hotspot finder, shown in Figure 10.2. These are pocket-sized devices that detect wireless hotspots. They can be purchased online or at local stores. Here are a few of the manufacturers:

- Canary Wireless—www.canarywireless.com
- IOGear—www.iogear.com
- Kensington—www.kensington.com

LINGO

Wi-Fi is technically the trademark for the certification of products that transmit data over wireless networks. It is commonly used as an abbreviation for wireless networking.

sandy's tip

If your portable computer doesn't have wireless connectivity built in, you can add it with a wireless card or USB adapter. Wireless cards are usually less obtrusive, so you may want to look at them first. Check out online discount retailers such as www.buy.com, or just visit your local electronics store.

■ Linksys—www.linksys.com

■ Trendnet—www.trendnet.com

Hotspot finders come in many shapes and sizes. The Kensington device can be attached to your keychain and can even detect Bluetooth wireless networks. Trendnet and Linksys have devices that combine a USB flash drive with a Wi-Fi finder.

When shopping for a hotspot finder, look for one that has an easily readable LCD screen and that shows the signal strength and encryption status. You will find many different varieties for less than $50.

FIGURE 10.2
The Canary wireless detector shows you the available hotspots.

Websites That List Hotspots

Be sure to use the Internet to make a list of available hotspots at your destination before you travel. JiWire (www.jiwire.com) is an excellent place to visit. Just click its Wi-Fi Hotspot Finder, as shown in Figure 10.3. This website allows you to search for free and pay hotspots and also lets you search by hotels, cafés, restaurants, airports, and bars.

Although JiWire lists more than 7,000 hotspots in the United States, it did not find many that I know are available in my own local area. Because hotspots are proliferating so quickly, it is always good to check a few websites to make sure you can find a hotspot in your area of choice.

Google (http://labs.google.com/location) also helps you find hotspots in airports, RV parks, hotels, and vacation rental properties. I find the Google interface a bit confusing. You need to put in a city, address, or zip code to get the map of your choice. Then you type "hotspot" to get a list of hotspots. Google aggregates the results from JiWire, Yahoo!, and several other hotspot finders.

Sandy's tip

As mentioned previously in this chapter, if you will be staying in a hotel, you can check with that hotel to see whether it has Internet access. Many hotels now offer free Internet access in the rooms, and some also offer it in the lobby and/or other public areas. The Wi-Fi Freespot Directory at www.wififreespot.com/hotels.html helps you find a hotel with free wireless service.

You may want to look for a hotel chain that you know has Internet connectivity available when you book your reservation. Geektools (www.geektools.com/geektels) lists many hotels that offer Internet access.

AnchorFree at http://anchorfree.com lists more than 10,000 locations that offer free wireless access. Another good choice for finding free Internet access is the Wi-Fi Free Spot Directory at www.wififreespot.com.

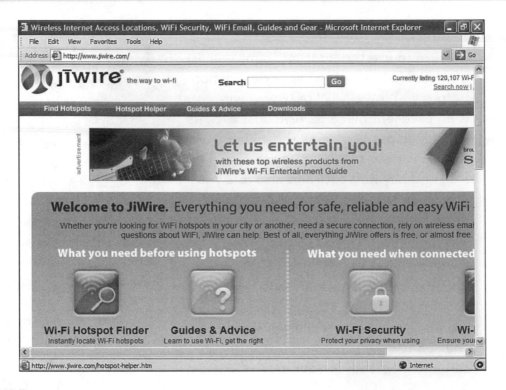

FIGURE 10.3
The Wi-Fi Finder on the JiWire website is an excellent resource for finding hotspots.

BLOOPER ALERT

As you search for hotspots, you will find that some sites are free and others charge you travel. JiWire (www.jiwire.com) is an an hourly or daily rate. It doesn't make much sense to pay for Internet access when you can get it for free. So you may want to check out the free wireless hotspots before you open your wallet at a hotspot that makes you pay.

Some Restaurants and Stores Offer Free Hotspots

It also pays to know that several chain restaurants and stores routinely offer free Internet access. Here are a few that you can find in many different areas across the country. Surf to their websites to find their exact locations and more information. The Panera Bread website is shown in Figure 10.4.

- Apple stores—www.apple.com/retail/

- Atlanta Bread Company—www.atlantabread. com

- Panera Bread—www.panerabread.com/wifi.aspx
- Schlotsky's restaurants—www.schlotzskys.com

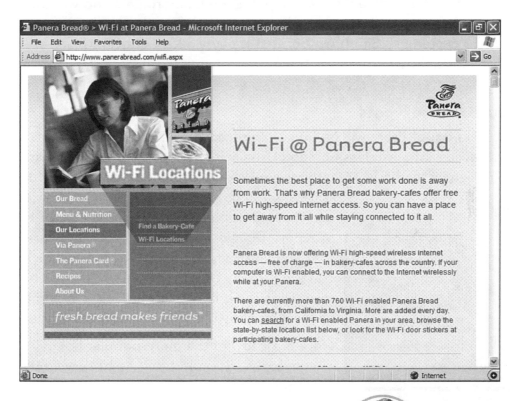

FIGURE 10.4
The Panera Bread website lists its many free Wi-Fi locations.

Also, when you travel, look for signs in restaurants, cafés, and coffee shops that indicate that they are a wireless hotspot. More establishments are becoming hotspots every day, and these places usually put a small sign on their door or front window.

BLOOPER ALERT
If you are using the free Internet access in a restaurant or coffee shop, be sure that you aren't hogging a table when customers are waiting to be seated. Some Panera restaurants request that you limit your time to 30 minutes between the hours of 11 a.m. and 2 p.m.

One of my favorite restaurants, Lucky 32 in Cary, NC, recently became a wireless hotspot. I passed through the doors several times before I realized it had become a hotspot. Even Laundromats and workout facilities are becoming wireless hotspots, and often these services are free to customers. So remember that it pays to look at every place you visit, especially when you are traveling.

Pay-for-Use Hotspots

No doubt there will be times when you will have to pay for Internet access at a wireless hotspot. Usually if a hotspot is free, it says so. If the sign instead says something like "Wireless service offered by T-Mobile," this means you have to pay an hourly or daily fee to use the Internet access. Services such as T-Mobile, Wayport, Boingo, and AT&T are hotspot services that you must pay for. If you will be doing a lot of traveling, it may be worthwhile to see which service covers the area you are traveling in and to purchase a monthly pass for that service.

Sandy's tip
T-Mobile is a cell phone provider as well as a hotspot provider. You do not have to use its cell phone service to sign up for its hotspot service.

BLOOPER ALERT
Most restaurants that are hotspots are for restaurant patrons, so go ahead and buy a cup of coffee or a sandwich while you surf.

Here are a few of the more popular hotspots that charge for service and the type of service they currently offer:

- Borders bookstores—T-Mobile
- FedEx Kinko's—T-Mobile
- McDonald's Restaurants—Most, but not all, are run by Wayport
- Starbucks coffee shops—T-Mobile
- UPS stores—Boingo

Deciding which service to purchase Internet time from in advance is more difficult than it sounds because there are several services of this type, and each has hotspots across the country. Service in airports is especially problematic. For example, you may be traveling from Love Field in Dallas, which uses T-Mobile service, to O'Hare International Airport in Chicago, which uses Boingo's service.

The previously mentioned JiWire website lists many airports and the type of service they use. You can also get information at each airport's website. You can find these most easily by entering the three-letter airport code and the word "airport" into any search engine. For instance, surf to the Google website at www.google.com and enter "ORD airport" to find information about Chicago's O'Hare. Enter "LAX airport" to pop up a link to the Los Angeles airport website.

If you want to subscribe to a wireless service before you leave home, be sure to investigate the service, charges, and coverage in detail, because each is different and all are somewhat complicated. Here are the websites for several of the most widely used wireless Internet service companies:

- Boingo—www.boingo.com

- T-Mobile—www.tmobile.com

- Wayport—www.wayport.com

Some services such as Boingo also include other types of paid services. For instance, if you sign up for a Boingo connection, you can also use it to access Wayport, AT&T, and Sprint hotspots. The Boingo website is shown in Figure 10.5.

Internet Access on the Road Without Computers

A mobile computer can get you on the Internet and be your traveling computer workbench, but there are several other ways to access the Internet while you are on the road.

Many of today's Personal Digital Assistants (PDAs) and cell phones can also help you get connected. To do this, you need a device that is Wi-Fi-enabled, and you have to pay an extra fee for Internet access to your cell phone service provider.

FIGURE 10.5
At the Boingo website you can sign up for service before you leave for your trip or anytime you are on the road.

Sandy's tip
The stronger the signal and the fewer people who are accessing the hotspot, the faster the service.

As soon as you have the right equipment and the necessary service, accessing the Internet and your email with a cell phone is easy, but it is not for everyone. If you are not comfortable reading a small screen and pressing tiny buttons, stick to a desktop or laptop computer for your Internet access.

Traveling with Your Laptop

A laptop computer is the ultimate productivity tool to keep you connected on the go.

How to Connect to the Internet on the Road

There are three ways to use your laptop computer to hook up to the Internet. The first is to use a dial-up connection, which uses an analog modem that is typically built into your computer. Keep in mind that this is the slowest method of communicating with the Internet, and you can incur hotel telephone charges or other long-distance charges when you use it. So I recommend it only if you cannot access the Internet through a broadband wired or wireless connection.

You can also use the Ethernet network port on your computer to hook up to a wired network. Although most newer hotels and motels are adding wireless networks, many older hotels still have wired broadband Internet access. To access a wired network, you simply insert one end of an Ethernet cable into your computer and the other into the network outlet.

Since wireless (Wi-Fi) access is expanding all over the world, it is currently the best and easiest way to access the Internet on the road. Most new portable computers have built-in wireless access. If you have an older laptop that doesn't have wireless capabilities, you can give it the ability to use wireless by purchasing a wireless card. For less than $50, your laptop instantly becomes wireless-enabled. The current Wi-Fi standard is called 802.11g. It is backward-compatible with the older 802.11b standard that is often found in hotels and wireless hotspots, so that is currently the best type

Sandy's tip

When you purchased your laptop, it probably came with a start-up disk to restore the hard drive to its initial state. It's a good idea to always travel with a copy of that disk in case you run into trouble. Also be sure to back up your work to a USB flash drive or CD before you leave, and as you work.

Sandy's tip

Almost all laptops have an Ethernet port that can be used to hook up to a wired network. Always carry an Ethernet cable just in case the hotel's Internet access is wired but a cable is not available.

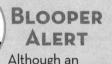

LINGO

Ethernet is the standard method of connecting a computer to a wired local-area network using a coaxial cable. The port on your computer looks similar to a telephone jack but is slightly larger.

BLOOPER ALERT

Although an Ethernet cable looks just like a telephone cable, the ends are a different size, and they are not interchangeable. Be careful to plug only an Ethernet cable into this port. Plugging in a phone line can damage your Ethernet card.

LINGO

SSID stands for Service Set Identifier. It the name assigned to a wireless network.

of card to purchase. A newer standard called 802.11n is also on the market, but as I write this the standard is still undergoing changes, so you won't want to purchase 802.11n equipment until the dust has completely settled. D-Link (www.dlink.com), Linksys (www.linksys.com), and Netgear (www.netgear.com) are three of the most popular makers of Wi-Fi cards.

If you are using Windows XP or Vista, it is easy to find out if a wireless network is in the area. Just click the computer icon that looks like a computer with three waves coming out of it on the right side of the taskbar at the bottom of the screen. Then choose "View Available Wireless Networks." If a wireless network is available in your location, it is listed. You simply highlight the connection and click the Connect button. Windows gives you the access point name (SSID) and tells you whether the access point is secure (you need a password and/or payment to connect) and if it is available. It also tells you the signal strength.

Mac users have it even easier. The Airport wireless card picks up any wireless signals and lists them in the Airport Signal menu at the top of the screen. Just select the wireless network that you want to use, and your computer connects automatically.

Cell phone companies now also offer mobile broadband cards that can be used in laptop computers to gain access to the Internet via their cell phone networks. You will have to pay a hefty monthly service charge for this service, but with this type of service you can access the Internet almost anywhere that you can use a cell phone.

Accessing Email

Finding a computer or Internet connection can be easy, but it is not always easy to access your email on the road. So always plan ahead. If you are still using a dial-up account for your Internet service and email, you can take your service provider's telephone number with you and hook up your computer to the telephone line to access the Internet and get your email.

However, there are easier ways to do this, without incurring extra telephone charges.

The easiest way to access email on the road is to use a Web-based email account such as Google's Gmail (www.gmail.com), Microsoft's Hotmail (www.hotmail.com), or Yahoo! Mail (http://mail.yahoo.com).

All your mail, your address book, and your archived email are kept online when you use a Web-based account. This makes it easy to access them from any Internet-connected computer anywhere in the world. With your account, you are given plenty of storage space for your email files. All of these services are free, with no hidden charges. Even if you have a regular email account that you received with your home or business Internet account, you can also keep a Web-based email account.

If you want to use the email account that came with your Internet service and it is not a Web-based email account, you can also use a Web service such as mail2web.com (http://services.mail2web.com) to check your email on the road. At mail2web.com you simply enter your email account and your password to access your email. The basic service is also free.

LINGO

Web-based email is a type of service that allows you to read, write, and store email on the World Wide Web. This type of email has its own interface that is similar to email programs such as Outlook Express, Thunderbird, and Eudora.

Sandy's tip

It is always wise to change your email password often—especially after a trip where someone may have seen you typing your information.

Laptop Safety

Portable computing is easy, and it keeps you in touch with family and friends no matter how far you travel. However, you must be careful to keep your laptop in tip-top condition.

The first thing to remember is that computers are delicate pieces of equipment that are sensitive to hot and cold. Don't leave your computer in a hot car in the summer or in the frigid cold in the winter. Constant humidity can also damage computer components.

Sandy's tip
Lightning can damage computers and other electronic equipment. When a storm is brewing, it is best to unplug your computer if possible.

You also need to protect your computer from power spikes and surges as well as lightning. This is especially important when you're traveling, because you don't know the status of the electrical supply or the condition of the power lines you're hooking up to.

Small power surges and spikes are a normal part of our electrical system. Sometimes electric lines are affected by larger power spikes that can damage computer equipment. A power surge, whether caused by lightning, construction, or some unknown event, can knock out various parts of a computer, including the motherboard, which is the heart of the computer. So don't take chances.

Portable surge protectors are available from many reputable companies, including APC (www.apc.com), Belkin (www.belkin.com), and TrippLite (www.tripplite.com). The ones I like the best are those that attach to the cord rather than to the outlet. These can be attached to your laptop cable, and you can forget that they are there. So you will never be without your power protection.

Sandy's tip
When traveling with a portable computer, it is always a comfort to use an in-room hotel safe to store your computer when you are out and about.

If you will be hooking your portable computer to a telephone line or an Ethernet port, be sure to purchase a surge protector that allows you to run the telephone and/or Ethernet cables through the surge protector. This gives your computer an added layer of protection from surges and spikes that can damage it through telephone or network lines.

Conserving Battery Power

Each new generation of computer chips and batteries extends the life of batteries. My first portable computer had a battery life of one hour. My newest one lasts about four hours. Yet, when I'm on an airplane or traveling, the battery never seems to last long enough.

One solution is to purchase a spare battery. If you use your computer a lot, this may be a viable option for you. However, if you're a just an average user, you may want to institute a few battery conservation habits instead.

BLOOPER ALERT

If you turn off the wireless connectivity to conserve power, be sure to turn it back on when you want to access the Internet.

Everything your computer does requires power. So reducing the number of procedures it performs conserves power. For instance, turn off your wireless card when it is not in use. If you leave it on, it is constantly searching for a wireless network and is using power to do so.

If you have added a wireless card to your computer, you can simply remove it. If your computer came with wireless built in, you can often turn it off with a small button or switch on the computer itself. If you don't see a switch, check the manual for its location or for information on how to turn off the wireless connectivity. Some computers have a shortcut key combination such as pressing the FN key plus F2 to shut down and restart the wireless connectivity.

Sandy's tip

When you need to conserve power, unplug any accessories that are attached to your laptop.

To conserve power, you will also want to limit activities such as using the DVD player or burner, which can use a lot of power. Some laptops also allow you to decrease the screen's brightness to save power. In Windows XP, click Start, Control Panel, and select Power Options. This area allows you to reduce the power consumption of many of your computer devices and also lets you power down the entire system.

With computers, cell phones, PDAs, digital music players, and digital cameras, it is easy to find that you are traveling with a gaggle of cords and chargers. If you find yourself in that situation, you may want to consider a universal charger like the iGo (www.igo.com) from Mobility Electronics, Inc. As shown in Figure 10.6, the iGo uses one device with interchangeable tips to charge all your devices. Some models can even charge more than one device at the same time. This device is especially nice because it works with AC outlets, automobile cigarette lighters, and airline power ports. Fellowes (www.fellowes.com) and Targus (www.targus.com/us) sell similar products.

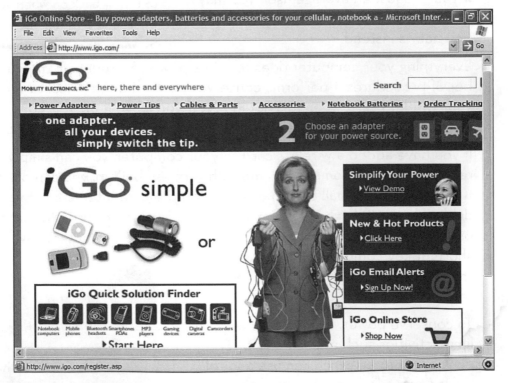

FIGURE 10.6
The iGo universal charger lets you leave some of those cords and cables at home.

Another option for recharging your smaller gadgets is to use the USB port on your notebook. Zip-Linq (www.ziplinq.com) has small, retractable cables that can be used for this purpose.

Preparing Your Equipment for Travel

A missing power cable or battery can make for a disastrous experience on the road. It can be difficult and expensive to try to replace a missing component, so it is important to be sure you pack everything you need for using your computer while traveling.

> **Sandy's tip**
> Always operate your laptop on a hard surface, preferably one that allows some ventilation. If you use it on your lap, be sure that your clothing is not blocking the air vents, causing it to overheat.

The best way to do that is to make a list of all the tasks you will want to use your computer for during the trip. You may want to access the Internet, check your email, work with certain documents, watch DVDs, or download pictures to email home. Make sure that your computer has all the software needed to perform these tasks. Then turn to the hardware.

It is easy to forget the batteries, a memory card, or a power cable. So set out everything before you leave. Gather your cell phone, computer, portable electronic games, digital music player, and any other electronic equipment you want to take along. Hook up each piece of equipment to make sure that you have everything you need. Be sure to include the chargers, batteries, cartridges, memory cards, and cables for each item.

Also check to make sure that you have the cables and other equipment necessary for any equipment you want to hook up to your computer. For instance, do you need a memory card reader or a cable to transfer pictures to your computer? Do you need a cable to update your MP3 music player?

> **Trivia**
> The most forgotten high-tech item is the charger for your cell phone.

If you need to take files with you on your trip, you can email them to yourself or put them on a USB flash drive. All computers less than five years old have a USB port that can accommodate these small devices. Plug one into your PC, and you see it as a drive in My Computer. On a Mac the drive instantly appears on your desktop. You can use it to transfer, back up, and carry your files with you.

Don't forget to label all your equipment before you leave home. A simple handheld labeler such as the Dymo Letra Tag (ωωω.δψμο.χομ) produces clean, clear labels for all your gear. Or you can get a Dymo or Brother (www.brother.com) label maker that attaches to your computer for even more personalized labels.

If you will be going through security at an airport, this is especially important. It is easy to be separated from your gear during a security check, and a simple label may be all you need to be reunited.

Travel Accessories Worth the Price

When you travel, little things can make a big difference. Accessories for your mobile computer and other electronic devices can keep them safe, make them more useful, and even add to your comfort while using them.

Carrying Cases

The first accessory you should consider is a case to hold and protect your portable computer. Whether you travel by RV or airplane, these cases can be a godsend. The type of travel you do and your personal preferences make a big difference in your choice of notebook totes. For instance, if you are constantly running from gate to gate at the airport and you have a bad back, a case on wheels may be perfect for you. Some people prefer to keep their load a little lighter by choosing cases that hold only the computer and cord. Others want a bag that can accommodate the computer, cord, files, and papers as well as other equipment.

Computer cases come in just about every size and shape imaginable. You can carry your computer in your hand, on your back, or on your shoulder, or take it along on wheels. You must remember two important things when choosing a case.

The first is your physical condition. Remember that most portable computers can be heavy. Even with the lighter models I find that my shoulders aren't as strong as they used to be, so I often opt for backpacks or bags on wheels. Assess your strength and needs carefully when choosing a case.

The second thing to consider is the amount of padding and security that the case offers. Computers need to be shielded from bumps and falls as well as from the elements. So the more protection you can give your computer, the better off you will be.

- Slappa (www.slappa.com) makes some well-padded bags with heavy-duty construction and industrial-strength zippers. My travel bag on wheels is a Slappa.

- Roadwired (www.roadwired.com) features Advanced Protection System laptop bags and cases that have padding plus high-tech protection against environmental pollutants and corrosion. I use a Roadwired R.A.P.S.! Advanced Protection Wrap for my expensive digital gear. This is a padded piece of fabric that has weather protection, shock absorption, and protection against corrosion. Just wrap it around your equipment for added protection.

- Waterfield Bags (www.sfbags.com), shown in Figure 10.7, are padded and well-designed, and many are customizable. They come in many different styles with insets of different colors. My Waterfield laptop sleeve is lightweight but offers padded protection whether I travel to Europe or the local coffee shop.

FIGURE 10.7
Waterfield's computer bags and pouches come in many shapes and sizes.

■ Mobile Edge (www.mobileedge.com) has a line of protective and well-designed backpacks, briefcases, and messenger-type bags. I am especially enamored of its TechStyle EVA cases, which are lightweight but made of a semi-rigid compression-molded EVA material. Its line of brightly colored computer portfolio cases is perfect for the woman on the go.

Sandy's tip
Be sure to shut down your computer before you take it for a long journey in its carrying case.

While you are investigating bags for your computer, don't forget about smaller pouches and pockets for your other electrical gear. A small durable pouch from SFBags (www.sfbags.com) keeps my iPod, charging cable, and earphones conveniently located and secure when I travel.

Fellowes (www.fellowes.com) and Targus (www.targus.com/us) sell similar products. With such a wide variety of bags, you are sure to find one that has the right features along with the needed portability and protection.

Accessorize for Ease of Use

Portable computers are convenient but not necessarily comfortable. A few well-chosen accessories can add to their ease of use and make your computing time on the road more comfortable.

Unless you happen to be one of the few people who enjoy using the touch pads and pointers on portable computers, a small portable mouse will be a welcome addition. These hook up easily to the laptop's USB port with no additional software necessary. Just plug them in, and they are ready to use. You can also add a cordless mouse for an even more freeing experience. Look at Logitech (www.logitech.com), Microsoft (www.microsoft.com), and Iogear (www.iogear.com) for a large variety of mini-mice that are laptop-friendly. Try Atek (www.atek.com) for a SuperMini Optical Mouse that is about the size of a tube of lipstick and can be used on the palm rest of most notebook computers.

Remember that your USB port can be used to power many small accessories that can be useful when you travel. These devices come in many shapes and sizes. Portable USB notebook lights and memory card readers make it easier to transfer the pictures from your camera to your computer. There are even portable USB devices that include fans to keep you cool and cup heaters to keep your coffee warm.

LINGO

Memory card readers are also called flash card readers. They are peripheral devices that usually attach to the computer via the USB drive. These devices let you insert the memory card from your camera, phone, or PDA and allow you to transfer the data without installing drivers or software.

Other useful accessories include portable keyboards. The Virtually Indestructible Keyboard from GrandTec (www.grandtech.com) is made of lightweight, water-resistant plastic and is extremely portable.

If you use your computer a lot when you travel, you may want to invest in a small stand that will make your computing more comfortable. The AVIATOR laptop (www.keynamics.com) stand is an inexpensive way to keep your laptop at the proper position and to keep the bottom from getting too hot. Many other types of laptop stands are available, but some are not too portable.

When looking for laptop accessories, if you can conceive it, you can probably find it. There are many interesting choices that you should investigate before you travel.

Laptops and Air Travel

I have already talked a little about many airports being hotspots. Internet access is no longer just a perk found in exclusive and costly airline member rooms. Now most large airports offer wireless connectivity. Unfortunately, most charge a fee, but $10 a day may be worth it when you have a three- or four-hour delay. Some airports also have "laptop alleys" where you can hook up your laptop to the Internet for shorter time periods. Many of these areas also have computers that you can rent.

Sandy's tip
Be sure to put your name, address, telephone number, and cell phone number on your laptop before you start your trip.

Other amenities such as battery-charging stations for laptops and kiosks for DVD rentals are starting to appear in many airports.

Internet connectivity is slowly becoming available on airplanes. It is a boon for bored travelers aboard long flights. I recently connected to the Internet on an SAS flight from Chicago to Stockholm. Internet access was accomplished by a satellite connection and was absolutely wonderful. Both European and U.S. power plugs were available in the armrests of the business and economy plus seats. Several payment plans were available so that you could pay for two hours, four hours, or the entire flight.

Right now only long-haul airlines are offering Internet service in the air, but U.S. airlines are poised to begin offering it in the near future. Check with your airline for information. For a complete listing of airline connectivity options plus a place to rent a computer for the ride, check out the Platypus computing Rental Services website at www.rentcomputers.com/sosair.html.

Outlets for recharging your laptop computer are beginning to be a rarity in airports. If you see an open outlet, grab it, but don't expect that one will always be available. Charge your laptop before you travel. If it is really important to work on your computer for a long period, bring a spare battery just in case.

Safe Surfing

An expensive notebook filled with personal data is a tempting target for thieves.

You need to protect the hardware by being sure to keep your computer in view and/or secured at all times when traveling. If you will be leaving your computer in a hotel room, secure it in an in-room safe or lobby safe. If safes are not available,

BLOOPER ALERT
If you use your laptop to watch DVDs in public places like airports and planes, be sure to bring a pair of headphones so that others don't have to listen to your movie .

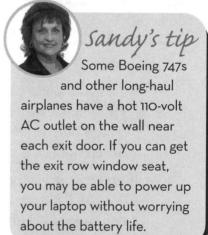

sandy's tip
Some Boeing 747s and other long-haul airplanes have a hot 110-volt AC outlet on the wall near each exit door. If you can get the exit row window seat, you may be able to power up your laptop without worrying about the battery life.

BLOOPER ALERT
When the drink service cart comes out, put away your laptop. Accidents and turbulence have been known to cause spillage that can adversely affect your computer.

purchase a cable lock. All laptops have a place where you can attach such a lock. Kensington (www.kensington.com), Targus (www.targus.com), and others have a large variety of cable locks, including keyed and combination lock models. You use the cable to lock your laptop to an immovable object.

LINGO

Encryption is a procedure that mathematically encodes data so that it can be read only by authorized users.

Remember that it is also important to secure your data. Always create a backup of your data in case your laptop is stolen or damaged. If you keep personal data on your computer, be sure to encrypt the files so that a thief cannot access them. Windows XP Professional, Windows Vista, and Mac OS X all let you encrypt files from the operating system interface. Unfortunately, if you use Windows XP Home Edition, you have to use third-party software to encrypt files.

Be sure to put a password on your operating system. This won't keep high-tech hackers from gaining access to your data, but it may stop an average person who picks up your laptop from seeing everything on your computer.

If you travel a lot, consider purchasing a laptop with a built-in fingerprint reader. If your fingerprint doesn't match one of those that have been registered in the computer, you can't log in.

Portable USB flash drives such as the SanDisk Cruzer Profile have a built-in fingerprint reader. This means that even if the drive is lost or stolen, the data on it is inaccessible.

For about $50 a year you can install software such as Absolute Software's Computrace (www.absolute.com), which can track down your computer when a thief uses it to log on to the Internet.

Online Overseas

Using your laptop overseas is easy as long as you come prepared. Usually you simply need a plug adapter like those sold by Belkin (www.belkin.com), Travel Oasis (www.traveloasis.com), and Kensington (www.kensington.com). These types of adapters allow you to plug your laptop into different types of power outlets. However, these adapters don't convert the power voltage. So, before you use one, you should always check the documentation that came with your laptop to see whether it can handle voltages found in other countries. Many times you will be able to look at the power block on your laptop cable, and it will state the voltages that it can handle. Most, but not all, of today's laptops can handle the 240V power used in much of the world, but you are wise to check it out before you plug it in.

To learn more about the electrical systems worldwide and get illustrations of the different types of electrical plugs you may encounter, check out the World Electric Guide at http://kropla.com/electric.htm. It gives extensive information on plug adapters, power converters, and surge suppressors.

Another good website for information on foreign electricity is the Voltage Valet at www.voltagevalet.com.

In many countries it is easy to find computer hookups and cybercafes. In more-upscale metropolitan areas, where most locals have computers in their homes, there are fewer cybercafes, but they are still available. On a recent trip, I found computers to use throughout Germany, Switzerland, and Sweden. Wireless hotspots are available in many countries. Just be sure to check out the charges before you hook up. A simple online search will give you information for the particular country you'll be visiting.

You can leave the United States with your laptop computer and other gear with no problem. However, when you return, you may be asked to prove that you purchased the equipment before you left the States. Although this has never happened to me, I have heard tales of woe from others. The U.S. Customs and Border Protection Agency has a useful publication called "Know Before You Go" on its website at www.cbp.gov/xp/cgov/travel/vacation/kbyg. You will want to check this out before you take any expensive equipment out of the country. Filling out a CF 4455 and having it certified will cover you, but currently this must be done in person at a Customs office or by a Customs official at an airport.

Sandy's Summary

The Internet has become such an integral part of our lives that we don't want to do without it when we go on the road. With today's services and technology, we don't have to.

If you don't want to carry a heavy laptop computer, you can hook up to the Internet at hotels, libraries, college campuses, and cybercafes almost anywhere in the world.

When you have a wireless-enabled portable computer, you can find hotspots in parks, restaurants, hotels, coffee shops, bookstores, and office supply stores. Many of these are free. Some charge a fee. But all allow you to get on the Internet for a quick email check or to browse for hours.

Don't worry. The Internet can help you find all the hotspots you need. Just use a search engine or a site that lists nothing but hotspots nationwide to look up the area where you will travel. You can find a hotspot before you leave or when you are on the road.

Using email on the road is easier than ever before, with Web-based email programs and services that let you access your email on the Web.

Using your laptop can be fun, but you need to be sure to pack carefully and to take good care of your laptop with accessories that protect it and make it easier to use.

Sandy Berger

Chapter 11

Don't Leave Home Without 'Em

Wandering reestablishes the original harmony which once existed between man and the universe.

—Anatole France

Today's high-tech devices make traveling easier and more comfortable. Whether you will travel by air or take to the roadways, you can try out many useful travel tools. Now that you have used online resources to save money on your airline tickets, hotel rooms, and car rentals, you might want to invest in a few high-tech devices that can make your trip more enjoyable. From digital music devices to language translators, these devices are must-haves for today's travelers.

Entertainment on the Go

When Sony introduced the first Walkman in 1979, millions started enjoying music on the go. Since then, choices for portable entertainment have grown considerably. Today we have tiny digital music devices and handheld gaming devices. We can even get music, games, and Internet entertainment on our cell phones. We are truly in a new world of on-the-go entertainment.

All this is great news for travelers. Although you may not play portable games or listen to digital music during an average day, these devices can really help pass the time when you're traveling.

Portable Digital Music Devices

Digital music devices are perfect for the traveler, because they come in small, easily portable sizes. Today the iPod (www.apple.com/ipod/), developed by Apple, is the most popular digital music device on the market.

Other popular digital music devices are called MP3 players named after the MP3 format, which is the most common file type for digital music.

There are three iPod models to choose from, the iPod Video (plays both audio and video files), iPod Nano, and iPod Shuffle. The iPod Shuffle, one of the tiniest digital music devices on the market, is 1.6 inches high, 1.07 inches wide, and only .41 inches deep. It weighs less than one-half ounce and clips onto your clothing or any other item for complete portability. The iPod Nano is only slightly larger, at 4.1 inches high, 2.4 inches wide, weighs in at 1.41 ounces and has an LCD screen for functionality. Finally the crème de la crème of iPod devices is the iPod Video, which plays both audio and video files and is roughly the size of a deck of playing cards.

The MobiBlu MP3 player is a bit larger than a sugar cube. Of course, there are many other music players available such as the Microsoft Zune (www.microsoft.com), Creative's Zen (www.creativelabs.com), the SanDisk Sansa (www.sandisk.com) , and the iRiver (www.iriver.com) four of the most popular MP3 players.

Free software such as Microsoft's Windows Media Player or Apple's iTunes is available for these devices. This software allows you to copy your CDs to your computer and then easily transfer the music to the portable device. You can also purchase music from an online music store such as iTunes or Rhapsody. Here are some of the more popular online music stores:

- AOL: http://music.aol.com

- eMusic: www.emusic.com

- iTunes: www.itunes.com

- MusicNet: www.musicnet.com

- Napster: www.napster.com

- Rhapsody: www.rhapsody.com

- Urge: www.urge.com

- Wal-Mart: www.walmart.com/music

- Yahoo Music: http://music.yahoo.com

BLOOPER ALERT

Remember that if you decide to purchase music online, the music from the iTunes Music Store works only on an iPod. Other online music stores, such as Napster, Rhapsody, and Urge, work only with certain music devices.

If your device is one of the newer models that includes a color screen and the capability to show photos or video, your options are broader. You can purchase movies and popular television programs and watch them on your digital music device.

Digital music devices range in price from $50 to $500. Shop carefully, because features and benefits vary greatly. Cheaper players have smaller storage capacities and no video capabilities. The larger the storage, the more you pay.

Headphones for Portable Devices

MP3 players come with headphones that allow you to listen to music or podcasts without disturbing others. Most devices come with headphones,

LINGO

Podcasting is a new method of distributing audio programming. A *podcast* is special broadcast content that is distributed over the Internet. Podcasting is a combo-word taken from "iPod" and "broadcast". You don't, however, have to use an iPod to listen to a podcast. You can listen on your computer or on any digital music player.

but for the most part they are in-the-ear (earphones) varieties with hard ends. I find these very uncomfortable, so I opt for headphones with soft caps that fit comfortably in the ear. They generally come with several different sizes of caps, so you can choose the ones that best fit your ears.

I wear soft-tipped in-the-ear headphones made by Apple (www.apple.com), but many others are available, including over-the-ear and in-the-ear models from Sony (www.sony.com), Sennheiser (www.sennheiser.com), and Etymotic (www.etymotic.com). You can even have in-the-ear headphones customized to your ear canal for added comfort, but they are pricey. You can also purchase "speaker pillows" that incorporate the speakers right in the pillow so you don't have to wear headphones at all.

If you travel by air a lot, you may want to try noise-canceling headphones. These generally cover your entire ear and drown out airplane noises quite easily. Models are available from Bose (www.bose.com), Koss (www.koss.com), and many other headphone manufacturers.

The HeadRoom website at www.headphone.com is a great place to visit for more information on headphones. Its product page (www.headphone.com/products) lists many different types of headphones, as shown in Figure 11.1. This site has a wealth of audio information, as well as a headphone selection guide and detailed technical information.

FM Transmitters for Portable Devices

If you are traveling by car, you can purchase an FM transmitter. Just plug your portable music device into one of these and tune both it and the car radio to an unused FM frequency. Your digital music plays through the car speakers. These devices range in price from $30 to $100 and are available from many different companies. These include

Griffin (www.griffintechnology.com) and DLO (www.dlo.com), which make iPod-compatible products, and Monster (www.monstercable.com/mp3), shown in Figure 11.2, which makes accessories for both the iPod and other MP3 players.

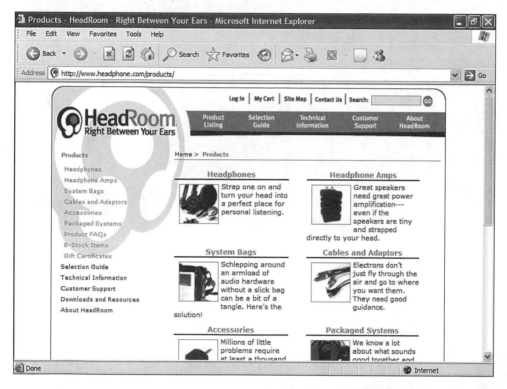

FIGURE 11.1
The HeadRoom website is filled with information that any headphone purchaser will find valuable.

When purchasing an FM transmitter for your car, shop around. Many options are available. Wireless units are even available, such as Griffin's iTrip for the Nano. Also be aware that many of these transmitters plug into your car's power outlet, so many of them charge your music player while it is plugged in. However, not all of them have this option. Be sure to read the details before you buy.

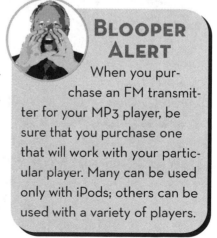

BLOOPER ALERT
When you purchase an FM transmitter for your MP3 player, be sure that you purchase one that will work with your particular player. Many can be used only with iPods; others can be used with a variety of players.

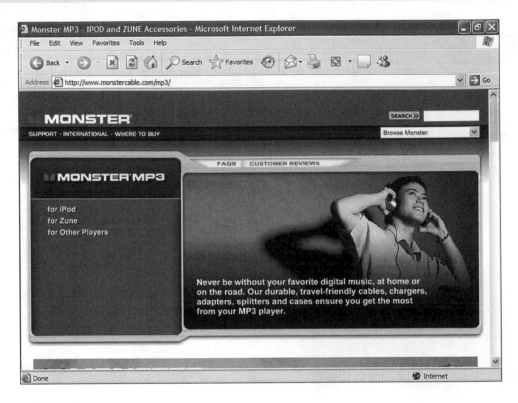

FIGURE 11.2
The MonsterCable website gives you an idea of the many accessories available for MP3 players.

Sandy's tip
Some MP3 players come with built-in voice recorders, which are perfect for making notes while traveling.

As these FM transmitters get more and more popular, manufacturers are adding even more features. For instance, Griffin's RoadTrip allows you to play the music on your iPod in the car, and then the removable transmitter can be attached to a PC or a Mac. This allows you to transmit the music that is on your computer to a nearby FM stereo, which could be useful in an RV or hotel room.

Travel Speakers for Portable Devices

Many companies also specialize in travel speakers for portable music devices. Some, like the Creative TravelDock (www.creativelabs.com), offer foldable speakers that are perfect for hotel rooms and RVs. If you are in the market for a new MP3 player and you like to listen to your music without headphones, be sure to look at some of the new models, such as Samsung's K5 (www.samsung.com), which has built-in speakers.

Portable Video Devices

When thinking about entertainment while you travel, don't forget about the many portable DVD players that are currently available. If you carry a laptop with you, you can always use it to play DVDs while in an airplane or hotel room. A portable DVD player for use in the car can be valuable if you don't carry a laptop. These players start at about $150. Those with larger screens and better clarity cost more. If you will have more than one person watching a portable DVD player in a public area like an airport or in a car where the rest of the family wants a little quiet, be sure to get a player that can accommodate two pairs of headphones.

sandy's tip
If you own a DVD player that has only one headphone jack, you can purchase a splitter at your local electronics store that allows two people to listen at once.

Handheld Game Devices

Although traveling is fun, delays can happen, and you need a little entertainment to help you pass the time. If you are waiting for a train or airplane, or you're just sitting in your hotel room alone, a little game-playing might be just what the doctor ordered.

My favorite handheld game is the Nintendo DS (www.nintendo.com/channel/ds), shown in Figure 11.3. Of course, you can play games on your cell phone, but if, like me, your aging eyes can't stand that small screen, this Nintendo will be perfect for you. Although the unit itself is only 5 inches by 2 ¼ inches by ¾ inches, it has two screens that are 2 ½ inches by 1 ¾ inches. One of these is a touch screen. This device also has speakers and a microphone.

FIGURE 11.3
The Nintendo DS is a portable gaming device that has many games for grownups.

Nintendo offers all types of games for the DS. Each game comes on a one-inch-square chip. One of the reasons that I like this gaming device is that Nintendo has created games that even those over fifty will love.

Nintendogs is a game that lets you adopt and train a puppy. Your dog reacts to you when you call him by name. You can use the stylus on the touch screen to pet your puppy. You can take him for a walk through the neighborhood, train him, and even enter him in competitions.

Another game called Brain Age was created by a neuroscientist with the express purpose of helping you keep your mind active and youthful. Other games for the Nintendo DS include Sudoku, card games, sports, and the ever-popular Mario games.

If you are into strategy or shoot-'em-up games, you may also want to investigate Sony's handheld PlayStation Portable (www.us.playstation.com/PSP). This device has great graphics on a small but adequate screen. Hundreds of PSP games are available.

If there is a game that you particularly like, you may also want to consider a small device dedicated to that game. You can get portable devices that play bridge, chess, FreeCell, Scrabble, Sudoku, and many other games.

A Nintendo DS or Sony PSP will set you back more than $100 plus the cost of games. If you don't want to spend that much, you have other options. One inexpensive handheld game I like for the whole family is 20 Questions. For less than $20 you get a small handheld device that seems to be quite intelligent. Think of any object, and the device asks you questions until it guesses the object you have chosen. It is surprisingly accurate and fun. 20Q Sports editions and 20Q Music editions are also available from Radica Games at www.radicagames.com.

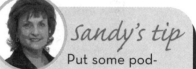

Sandy's tip
Put some podcasts or audiobooks on your MP3 player, and you won't have to drag along newspapers or books.

Traveling with Your Computer

Traveling with your computer can keep you connected and make traveling more fun. You can carry many small devices with you to make using your computer on the road easier. The following sections describe a few of them.

Sandy's tip
For more travel gadgets and information, visit the travel section of my Compu-KISS website at www.compukiss.com/travel, or see *Sandy Berger's Great Age Guide to Gadgets and Gizmos* (ISBN 0-7987-3441-9).

Portable Mice and Keyboards

With the popularity of portable computers, manufacturers are scampering to produce portable devices that can make using

LINGO

Bluetooth is a wireless technology for short-range wireless transmissions. It is often used for headphones for cell phones and in wireless mice and keyboards.

a laptop easier. For instance, portable mice and keyboards come in many different shapes and sizes.

If you hate using the touch pad on your laptop, it's easy to add a mouse. Just about any USB mouse will work, but if you travel a lot, you may want to find a small, portable mouse. The Atek Super Mini Mouse (www.atek.com) is compact and accurate. It is about the size of a tube of lipstick and comes in several colors for about $30. Logitech (www.logitech.com) has mice for notebooks in many different sizes, shapes, and prices. It even has a cordless optical notebook mouse that can wirelessly hook up to a Bluetooth-enabled laptop.

The MoGo mouse (www.newtonperipherals.com) is a $69 laptop mouse. As shown in Figure 11.4, this mouse is wireless and folds flat to fit in the laptop's PCMCIA card slot, where it can be stored and recharged at the same time.

LINGO

A **PCMCIA card** is also called a PC card. It is a credit-card-sized removable card for computers. Most laptop computers have a slot that accommodates these cards.

Like mice, portable keyboards come in many shapes and sizes. Fellowes (www.fellowes.com) has a Stowaway keyboard that folds up when not in use. Many other companies have similar products. If you are really hard on your keyboards, you also might investigate GrandTec's Virtually Indestructible Keyboard (www.grandtec.com), which is a lightweight full-size keyboard that can easily be thrown in a suitcase without fear of damage.

Wireless Connections

If your laptop is wireless-enabled, you will no doubt look for wireless networks to hook up to during your travels. Although you can turn on your computer and let it automatically find the wireless networks in the neighborhood, it is often inconvenient to have to drag out your computer and wait for it to boot up. An easier way is to use a small device called a Wi-Fi finder. I use a $60 Canary Hotspotter (www. canarywireless.com), shown in Figure 11.5. It shows you the wireless networks in the area, signal strength, and whether the network is encrypted. Kensington (www.kensington.com) and IOGear (www.iogear.com) have similar products.

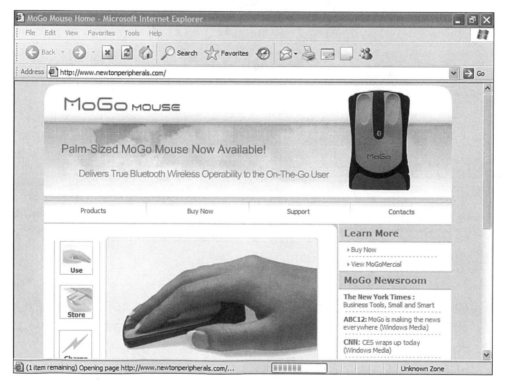

FIGURE 11.4

The MoGo mouse is an unusual but effective portable mouse.

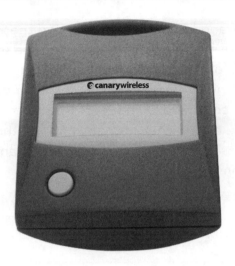

FIGURE 11.5
This small Canary device finds nearby wireless networks.

Portable USB Drives

A wonderful addition to any laptop computer is a USB flash drive, also called a USB key, pen drive, or thumb drive. This device is small enough to fit on your keychain or in your pocket. These drives can easily store and/or transport your data.

To use one, you simply insert it into your computer's USB port. Then click My Computer or Computer. The flash drive appears as a removable drive. You can simply drag the files between the flash drive and your computer to copy them.

Flash drives are great for taking your files and data with you when you travel, especially when you don't want to lug along a laptop. Some flash drives, like the SanDisk Cruzer Profile, have a built-in fingerprint reader that lets you encrypt your files so that no one else can access them if the drive is lost or stolen.

There are even flash drives that let you take all your data with you so that you can use any computer on the road as if it were your own. The Migo (www.migosoftware.com) is one such product. Not only does the Migo hold your data, but it synchronizes your data when you get back home with any changes you made while on the road. Migo also encrypts everything and doesn't leave any traces of your visit on the computers you use, so you can surf and do email on public computers in complete safety. Another similar solution is called U3. Information is available at www.u3.com, as shown in Figure 11.6.

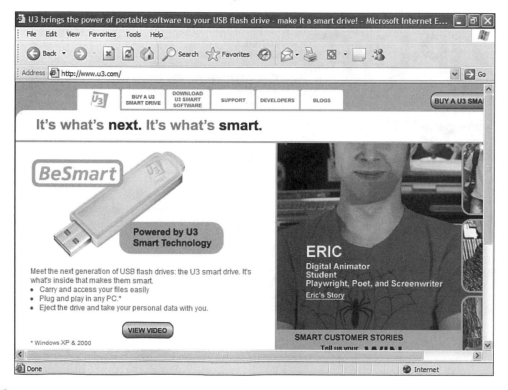

FIGURE 11.6
The U3 flash drive lets you take all your personal files with you without having to lug a laptop.

Specialty Cables

If you have ever struggled with tangled wires when you travel, you might like the Zip-Linq cables (www.ziplinq.com). The retractable cables are sturdy, take up less space, and pack well. As shown in Figure 11.7, there is a small circle of wire in the middle, and you simply pull from both sides to extend the wire. Another tug on each end retracts the wire when you are finished using it. A large variety of cables are available, including USB cables, Firewire cables, earbuds, and telephone chargers. Most cables cost between $6 and $12.

FIGURE 11.7
Zip-Linq cables save space and don't get tangled, because they are retractable.

Laptop Safety

If you travel with a laptop, you should keep it safe and secure. If you leave your laptop in a hotel room that doesn't have a safe, you will want to use a cable lock such as the Kensington MicroSaver Portable Notebook Combination Lock. Similar products are available from

Kensington (www.kensington.com) and Compucage (www.compucage. com). When the lock and cable are attached to the computer and an immovable object, they protect your computer from casual thieves. These locks can be found as key locks as well as combination locks. But be forewarned. None of these locks will deter a really smart thief who is bent on stealing your laptop, so get some insurance, encrypt important data, and always leave a backup of your data at home.

Power Adapters

When you carry multiple electronic devices, recharging them and carrying all those power adapters can be burdensome. A company called iGo (www.igo.com) has the answer. It provides one power adapter that, with the addition of different tips, can power many different devices. You can even use the iGo car adapter to recharge your equipment while on the road.

From about $100 on up, iGo even has chargers that recharge several devices at the same time. Its $25 iGo powerXtender battery-operated charger lets you power and charge your gadgets using four AA batteries. This could be a lifesaver for digital cameras that have proprietary battery packs.

Handheld Computing Devices

One thing to note here is that some PDAs, the BlackBerry, and cell phones are getting to be almost as smart as computers. With many of them you can surf the Web, take pictures, and play music. You can also add much functionality to these devices. For instance, the WorldMate software (www.mobimate.com) turns your PDA, BlackBerry, or phone into a valuable travel mate. You can use the software to get flight status updates, world clocks, currency converters, clothing size converters, weather forecasts, and many other travel tools.

You can also add GPS functionality to many cell phones, PDAs, and the BlackBerry. Although the screen on most cell phones is too tiny to make this function viable for this baby boomer, I find that an Internet-connected PDA with software and a GPS system is a valuable tool for travel.

Photographic Tools

You already know that digital cameras and camcorders are perfect for creating memories of your travels. Which type of camera you use depends on your experience, the amount of time and effort you want to put into your photos, and the amount of money you want to spend.

LINGO

SLR or **single-lens reflex** cameras are so called because they use a reflecting mirror when the shutter is released.

The two types of digital cameras that you will probably consider are the small point-and-shoot cameras and the larger and pricier SLR (single-lens reflex) cameras.

Point-and-shoot cameras let you quickly take a photo without worrying about the settings. There are settings you can adjust, but you cannot use additional lenses. An SLR camera lets you adjust settings to your heart's content. You can also change lenses to give yourself even more options. One of the biggest benefits of SLR digital cameras is that they don't have the shutter lag that plagues point-and-shoot digital cameras. If you have ever pressed the shutter and waited a few seconds for the picture to be taken, you have encountered shutter lag.

LINGO

Shutter lag is the delay between when you press the button to take a picture and when the camera actually takes the picture.

Nothing is more fun than using a digital camera on the road. The problem is, what do you do with those great pictures to make sure they get back home safely?

You should consider purchasing additional memory cards for your camera so that you don't have to erase old pictures to make room for new ones. If you are traveling with your laptop, you can use a device called a card reader to copy your pictures to your laptop. Card readers are inexpensive devices that hook up to the USB port on any computer. You purchase one that is made for the type of memory card your camera uses. The memory card reader appears as a device in My Computer (or Computer), where you can simply copy it to your computer. Card readers are available from many manufacturers, including Belkin (www.belkin.com), IoGear (www.iogear.com), and others.

If you are visiting relatives or attending a special celebration, you might want to look into portable printers that allow you to print your photos on the go. They are not as expensive as you may think. Some deliver excellent photo printing for less than $100. Check out Hewlett Packard at www.hp.com, Epson at www.epson.com, and Lexmark at www.lexmark.com.

> **BLOOPER ALERT**
>
> Don't get hung up on megapixels. A simple 3-megapixel camera is adequate for most photography. You need more only if you want to create large-format (such as poster-size) or more-detailed (close-up) photographs.

You may also want to look at the new devices that are called photo viewers. Although these are pricier than most printers or scanners, they are extremely portable and have screens where you can view the photos. Most also offer several gigabytes of storage space. They are perfect for viewing and storing your photos on the road. Look for many different versions from the printer manufacturers just mentioned.

Devices for International Travel

Traveling to far-off lands can be a real adventure, and it pays to be ready. Some high-tech devices can make the transition to different parts of the world easier.

Power Converters

As you know, not all countries use the same type of power. The standard in the U.S. is 110 volts. In Europe outlets are 240 volts. Two components are involved in power conversion: the adapter (plug) and the transformer, which handles the voltage.

Most newer devices work with either 110 or 220 volts. The power block on most laptops tells you how many volts the laptop can handle. If the power block doesn't give that information, consult the manual or the manufacturer's website for that information.

If your device can handle only 110 volts, you will need a transformer. If your device or the documentation states that it can handle 220 volts, you don't need a transformer.

In either case, you will need an adapter. Because the number and size of the prongs on the plugs vary from country to country, this adapter is necessary to plug in your equipment. The adapter attaches to the plug and transforms it into the type of plug used in the country you will visit. You need to learn what type of plug you need.

Also be aware that many power converters (transformers) are designed to work with high-voltage appliances such as hair dryers and irons. Low-voltage appliances such as small radios, alarm clocks, and PDAs may require a special converter.

BLOOPER ALERT

Even though the plug on your device may fit the outlet, the incorrect voltage may damage your equipment. Always check the voltage as well as the plug type.

Companies like American Power Conversion (www.apc.com) and Targus (www.targus.com) offer power converters. Franzus (www.franzus.com) offers a special converter that determines the voltage needed and auto-switches between high- and low-voltage equipment. The Franzus website also has a Voltage/Adaptor Guide, a Guide to Electricity, and an Adaptor Plug Guide (as shown in Figure 11.8) that help you determine all your power needs for international travel.

Cell Phones

Although some cell phones work in other countries, many do not. Even if your cell phone will work, you may not want to incur the sometimes-excessive charges for its use in other countries. One solution is a set of two-way radios commonly called walkie-talkies. These are nothing like the cans attached by string that you may have played with as a child.

Walkie-talkies have truly entered the high-tech world. Some are as light-weight and easy to carry as cell phones, and the average ones can have a range of about 12 miles. These devices are great for staying in touch with your companions during an international trip. They range in price from $50 to $120. Motorola (www.hellomoto.com) has several models to choose from.

FIGURE 11.8
The Franzus website has information on electricity, adapters, and voltage, which can be invaluable for international travel.

If your cellular service includes walkie-talkie service like Nextel, you may be able to use your cell phones as walkie-talkies. Some of these walkie-talkie phones even have International Direct Connect, which can be used to keep in touch from country to country. Check with your cellular provider to see how your hardware and service plan work.

Sandy's tip
Before you leave for an international trip, be sure to call your cellular service provider to activate international calling, if available, and to check on pricing.

Language Translators

Need to communicate with someone who doesn't speak English? You may want to carry a language translator. These small devices contain translations for thousands of commonly used phrases. Sharper Image (www.sharperimage.com) has a nice variety of handheld translators that range in price from $40 to $200. Many of these translators pronounce the words for you, which is invaluable when you're dealing with an unknown language. Translators like this usually work for the more common languages. I have seen them for English, Spanish, German, Russian, Dutch, Swedish, Italian, French, Portuguese, Turkish, Japanese, Greek, Hebrew, and Mandarin (Chinese).

Car and RV Travel

Hitting the road can be fun, but being prepared for emergencies should always be part of your plan. Several high-tech tools will keep you on the road and make your trip as void of problems as possible.

Tire Pressure Gauge

When you are on the road, even the little things can be important. For example, automotive experts will tell you that keeping your tires properly inflated saves you on gas and keeps your vehicle safer.

I don't know about you, but I have never been taught to read a tire pressure gauge. Yet this is the tool you need to keep your tires properly inflated. That's why I was impressed with the talking tire gauge by Measurement Specialties (www.msiusa.com). This $15 device has a nice handgrip. Just align the nozzle on the tire gauge with the valve stem on the tire. The reading is digitally displayed and spoken in a clear, computerized voice. This little tool makes it easy to check your tires while traveling.

Radar Detector

Radar detectors have long been used to detect radar on the road. As with many other gadgets, these devices have gotten better and better.

Some even use Digital Signal Processing to provide maximum range with minimum false alarms. Ranging from $80 to $400, these devices have a plethora of up-to-date features. The $340 Escort Passport from Sharper Image (www.sharperimage.com) is a typical feature-laden model that can even detect lasers.

BLOOPER ALERT

Some states prohibit radar detectors. Watch for signs as you enter the state, or check the state's chamber of commerce or visitor bureau website before you leave home.

Battery Charger

Another Sharper Image product, the Jump-Start DC Power Plus, is a useful tool on the road. It is a triple-duty product. It charges a car battery in minutes without jumper cables; it provides a portable power source for cell phones, laptops, and other devices; and it is a super-bright LED flashlight. The Jump-Start can be charged in a car's DC power socket or an AC outlet. You can see it at www.sharperimage.com/us/en/catalog/product/sku__AU400. Figure 11.9 shows a sneak peak.

Other Gadgets for Road Travel

As you surf the Web, you will find many different gadgets and gizmos that can make your time on the road safer and more comfortable. I'll tell you about just a few.

The Driving Mirror (www.maxiaids.com) is a special clip-on mirror that provides a clear view as wide as your car's rear window. At less than $20, it is perfect for giving you greater vision and more confidence when backing up and viewing cars and other objects in your rearview mirror.

How about a device to keep you a little better organized? For less than $10 the Sticky Pad (www.handstands.com) adheres to your dashboard and allows other things to adhere to it. It is perfect for holding your cell phone, keys, or music players, because they are in clear view and are easy to grab when you need them.

FIGURE 11.9
The Jump-Start DC Power Plus can jump your car, recharge your handheld devices, and light your way.

If you or someone you travel with has difficulty getting into and out of the car, the $25 Swivel Seat Cushion from Gold Violin (www.goldviolin. com) may be perfect. The seat cushion is a thin round polyfoam pad on a flexible plastic swivel base. Just put it in the car and sit on it. The base turns 360 degrees, making it much easier to get out of the car without straining your back or hips.

Of course, MP3 players are perfect for use in the car when paired with the FM transmitters that we talked about earlier in this chapter.

Another way to get music into your life when traveling by car is to use a satellite radio. The programming for satellite radio is beamed up to satellites and then back down. This means that you can listen to the same radio station on a car trip from New York to California. The variety is wonderful. You can pick up sports, traffic, talk radio, and specialty stations that include just about every genre of music.

The two popular satellite radio providers are Sirius (www.sirius.com) and XM (www.xmradio.com). There is a cost for the hardware, which includes the receiver and an antenna, as well as a monthly service charge of about $15. You can purchase satellite radio preinstalled on your car, truck, or RV, or you can use a portable satellite radio device. Many of the portable devices can go from your car to your home or hotel room.

If you are traveling by car or RV, a GPS (global positioning system) may be a good investment. These devices can also be purchased preinstalled in your car or RV, but you can also add them later. The GPSs you will want for your vehicle are the kind that show you a map of where you are and where you're going. They also give you verbal turn-by-turn instructions. They pinpoint your location by satellite and give you directions from their database of information. They are perfect for the traveler who hates to get lost but who can't stand to ask for directions.

My favorite in-car GPS is the TomTom Go (www.tomtom.com, shown in Figure 11.10). Other excellent manufacturers are Garmin (www.garmin.com) and Magellan (www.magellangps.com). Expect to pay several hundred dollars for a good GPS for your vehicle.

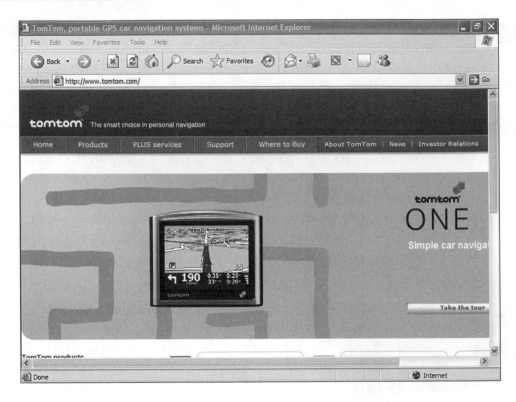

FIGURE 11.10
The TomTom website provides many different types of GPSs.

Air Travel

Air travel is often the fastest way to get to your destination, but it poses its own unique set of aggravations and inconveniences. High-tech gadgets come to the rescue in many of these situations.

Devices for Comfort

I always get a stiff neck when I travel by air. However, I have been able to eliminate my pain by using a travel pillow. My favorite travel pillow is the Tempur-Pedic (www.tempurpedic.com), which is made from vis-coelastic foam. This material was developed at NASA's Ames Research Center and is used in the seats of the space shuttle to improve seat cushioning and comfort and to provide crash protection. This foam is so technologically advanced that it has been inducted into the U.S. Space Foundation's Space Technology Hall of Fame. The first time you touch this pillow, you know that it is different. It feels as though there is gel in the material itself. This gel-like quality adjusts and molds to your head and neck contours, providing a comfortable and supportive pillow. At about $80, these pillows are pricey, but perfect for travel. They come in different shapes. I especially like the one that cradles your neck.

A less expensive choice is the pillow that my husband prefers, the FOM pillow by Brookstone (www.brookstone.com). It has thousands of soft microbeads encased in stretchable nylon. This pillow comes in a travel case, and it (or similar pillows) can often be found for sale in most airports.

If you have trouble sitting for long periods of time and are faced with a long fight, you may want to invest in a product like Magellan's (www.magellans.com) "Best Seat." Although it costs $225, it is a state-of-the art device that uses alternating pressure-point technology and a pump-and-valve system to "lift and shift the areas of your body that come in contact with the airline seat so your circulation is constantly enhanced."

Luggage

Another inconvenience of air travel is the shoulder pain you get from lugging heavy bags. This is not one of the joys of growing older, and it can be alleviated with the right luggage. You can purchase luggage on rollers that can fit under the seat or larger bags that go in the overhead bin. One of my favorite computer bags has become the four-wheeled Samsonite (www.samsonite.com) bag that fits under an airplane seat. Some other good manufacturers that make bags for computers and other equipment are Slappa (www.slappa.com), Waterfield (www.sfbags.com), and Targus (www.targus.com).

If you don't want to invest in new luggage, you can turn your old luggage into rolling luggage by purchasing a foldable set of wheels that attach to your luggage. Magellan's Travel Supplies (www.magellans.com)

has a nice variety of lightweight luggage and travel gear of this type. Its Luggage area at www.magellans.com/store/Luggage?Args= also has great information, including an Airline Carry On Guide, Which Bag Is Best, and How to Avoid Excess Baggage Fees. These are shown in Figure 11.11.

FIGURE 11.11

The Magellan's website has great articles on traveling by air and on related products.

When looking for a travel bag, you might also want to try backpacks. I find them inconvenient for air travel because you have to remove them when you sit down in the airport. But they are easier on the back and shoulders than many other types of bags.

An unusual but useful solution to the "How can I carry all this stuff?" dilemma when traveling by air is the SCOTT eVEST (www.scottevest. com). As shown in Figure 11.12, SCOTT eVEST offers jackets as well as vests.

FIGURE 11.12
The SCOTT eVEST lets you carry all your medicine, gadgets, and other paraphernalia in as many as 52 different hidden pockets.

These garments look like regular vests or jackets, but they have hidden pockets. Some have as many as 52 hidden pockets. These garments are made for gadget gurus, but I find that they are also perfect for travel, especially air travel. You can load the pockets with all the essentials you must carry. There is even a jacket that has a pocket large enough for a laptop computer. These jackets distribute the weight so that your back and shoulders are less prone to strain. Another benefit is that when it is time to go through security, you can simply remove the jacket and put it on the X-ray belt.

BLOOPER ALERT
Luggage differs greatly in weight. Some of the new lightweight materials can make your bag 40% lighter than similar bags. So always look for the lightest and sturdiest bag you can find.

Sandy's Summary

Today's gadgets and gizmos can make travel more comfortable and fun. Because you saved money by booking your travel online, you might want to splurge on some of these new devices that can help you get organized, stay entertained, and make you more comfortable.

There is no doubt that today's digital music players and DVDs provide entertainment while traveling. Whether you are in a car, on a plane, or on a ship, they can help you pass the time as well as make your travel experience more enjoyable.

Be sure to look for the accessories for MP3 players that can let you listen to your music in your car or hotel room. Many options are available.

Whatever you do, don't miss out on the fun that handheld gaming devices can provide. You don't want to miss the travel sights, but there are always downtimes in your hotel room or at the airport when these fantastic devices can help you pass the time enjoyably.

Many tools are available to help you travel with your computer and other digital devices. Whether you need a portable mouse or an electrical adapter, these devices are all available at your fingertips through the Internet.

Don't forget the many photographic tools available, as well as those simple devices that help you get up in the morning and keep you organized.

Yes, these high-tech tools are sure to help you enjoy your travels more. So don't leave home without 'em!

Sandy Berger

Chapter 12

Sharing Memories from Your Travels

Wandering reestablishes the original harmony which once existed between man and the universe.

—Anatole France

I can remember sitting through boring Super 8 movies and slide shows years ago as recently returned-home family members shared their vacation memories. I'm sure you can too. By the time the projector and screen were set in place and properly adjusted, most of us were ready to go home. What should have been a happy endeavor was often a chore for both the presenters and the viewers.

Times have certainly changed. Now sharing the memories of your trip can be a vibrant experience for both you and your loved ones. There are many exciting new ways to share your travel experiences with others, such as a blog or photo journal. You can email photos or create photo postcards. Or, when you get home, you can wow your friends and neighbors with an exciting presentation right on your computer or television.

In This Chapter

- Digital Photographic Memories That Last Forever
- Taking Great Vacation Photos
- Photo-Sharing and Photo-Printing Services Online
- Travel-Focused Photo-Sharing Websites
- Online Travel Journals (Blogs)
- Sharing Your Memories When You Get Home
- Other High-Tech Ways to Share Your Travel Photos

Digital Photographic Memories That Last Forever

When you travel, photo opportunities abound as you try to capture the moment for posterity. Digital cameras have made photography both more affordable and more fun. With a digital camera you can see the photo right after you snap it, so you can immediately retake any photos that are not quite right. You never have to look for a camera store to purchase film or take your film in for processing. Digital photography makes preserving memories of your travels easier than ever before.

Taking Great Vacation Photos

Even if you are an amateur photographer, it's easy to get your camera to capture the moment just as you remember it. Internet resources can help you get ready for your trip with great photography tips. The Fodor's Focus on Photography section (www.fodors.com/focus) is filled with tips and tricks for creating perfect travel pictures. This site has photography information that is relevant to both analog (film) and digital photography. The Classic Vacation Shots section gives tips on photographing your cruise, shooting from the air, and taking pictures of parades and fireworks displays. It even has information on taking pictures at zoos and aquariums, shown in Figure 12.1. There are some tips on taking silly pictures that show what an inventive photographer you are and how much fun that trip really was.

Not to be outdone by Fodor's in the photography area, Frommer's also has travel photography tips at www.frommers.com/tips/photography. Although it has some articles and an extensive photo gallery, the star of the photography area is the message board on cameras, phones, and gadgets (www.frommers.com/cgi-bin/WebX?14@@.ee97475). It's a great place to get your photography questions answered.

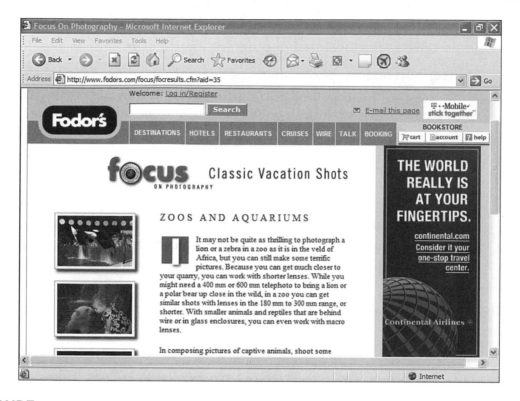

FIGURE 12.1
The Fodor's Focus on Photography website will have you creating travel pictures like a pro in no time.

If you are looking for answers to questions on photographing your trip, the SoGoNow.com website has a ton of questions and answers at www.sogonow.com/archives/travel_tips_and_resources/photo_tips. You can read about others' quest for knowledge in this area or ask your own questions.

For a plethora of Photo Tips, try the PhotoSecrets website at www.photosecrets.com. It gives you explicit information on how to take better photos in the Photo Tips area (www.photosecrets.com/tips.html). It lists 10 tips for travel photographers and contains many useful articles.

BLOOPER ALERT

Always keep an extra copy of your digital photos on a CD, DVD, or other external media. Hard drives can, and often do, crash.

If you are at all interested in postcard photography, this section also has some outstanding postcard photography and tips from their creators.

Shutterfly, a popular photo-sharing and photo-printing website, also is a helpful place to learn about travel photography. www.shutterfly.com/foley_tips/travel.jsp features photo tips from Pulitzer Prize-winning photographer Bill Foley.

The quest for good photographs may also lead you to the BetterPhoto.com website at www.betterphoto.com. BetterPhoto tries to sell you on its online photography courses. I can't attest to the quality of these courses, but I can recommend its free resources. Click Resources, as shown in Figure 12.2, and then choose from a list of informative articles and reviews. This site also has free photography newsletters.

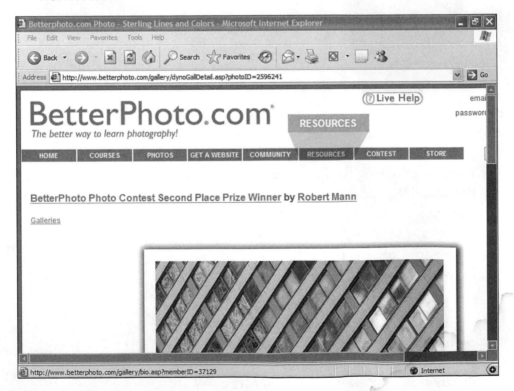

FIGURE 12.2
The Resources area of BetterPhoto.com has many free articles and reviews to help you improve your photographic skills.

If you are in the market for a new digital camera, the BetterPhoto.com website has digital camera comparison charts. It also has two very interesting Digital Camera Calculators. The first lets you select a camera by choosing the photos that illustrate your interests, goals, and values. The other is a digital camera calculator that lets you answer 10 questions to determine which digital camera is right for you.

After you narrow down your choices, you will want to visit Steve's DigiCams at www.steves-digicams.com for an in-depth review of the cameras you are considering.

Sandy's tip
Read the manual and learn to use your camera before your trip. When that perfect photo moment occurs, you'll be glad you did.

BLOOPER ALERT
Be sure to type the Web address carefully. Steve's DigiCams at www.steves-digicams.com gives you great information on digital cameras. A copy-cat website at www. stevedigicam.com just wants to sell you a camera.

Photo-Sharing and Photo-Printing Services Online

After you learn how to use your digital camera, you will want to share your photos. An online photo website is the perfect way to show off photos from your trip.

Finding a photo-sharing website is easy, but so many are available that you will probably want to take your time and survey some of the choices before you make a final choice. Although you can do this after your trip, it is a lot more fun to have the website in place and quickly upload your photos when you return. In fact, if you have your photo website in place, you can even upload pictures as your trip progresses by using your laptop computer, Internet cafés, or other computer resources.

Free Photo Services Sites

Many free websites let you upload your photos to display and share with others. Here are some of the more popular ones:

- Club Photo: www.clubphoto.com
- Flickr: www.flickr.com
- ImageEvent: http://imageevent.com
- Kodak EasyShare Gallery: www.kodak.com
- Picturetrail: www.picturetrail.com
- Picasa Web Albums: http://picasa.google.com
- Shutterfly: www.shutterfly.com
- Smugmug: www.smugmug.com
- Snapfish: www.snapfish.com

sandy's tip

Although online photo websites are an excellent place to share your photos, you always want to keep copies on your computer. Alternatively, storing photos on a CD or DVD is a great way to keep your hard drive space free and keep your treasured memories safe.

Each of these photo-sharing websites has its own unique personality and enables you to perform different tasks in different ways. So it is best to investigate as many as you can to assess the strengths and weaknesses of their features and how they compare against your likes and dislikes.

All of these sites let you post your pictures by creating personal online photo albums. Most have tools that allow you to easily upload your images to the website. Many allow viewers to make comments on the photos. Some, like Flickr, shown in Figure 12.3, even allow you to upload photos from an Internet-enabled cell phone.

FIGURE 12.3
The Flickr website lets you store, search, sort, and share your photos.

Many of these websites, such as Club Photo, EasyShare, and Flickr, offer free basic services and have upgraded services that they charge for. These services often include photo printing and special gift items personalized with your photos. For example, the free membership at Club Photo gives you unlimited photo sharing, 20 free 4×6-inch prints, and additional prints for 19 cents each. Platinum members get 4×6-inch prints for 17.1 cents each. The Kodak EasyShare Gallery gives you a free photo-sharing account with 10 free prints. These special offers are constantly changing, so be sure to read the fine print and try out the service before you decide which one to use.

Google's Picasa Web Albums is one of my favorites for posting and sharing photos. It works with Google's free Picasa software, which is available at the Picasa home page at http://picasa.google.com. Picasa is software that lets you organize and edit your photos. When you sign up for the free Web Album service, you can create online photo albums with one click from within the Picasa program. It makes organizing and sharing photos really easy. As shown in Figure 12.4, you can learn more about Picasa Web Albums at the Picasa home page.

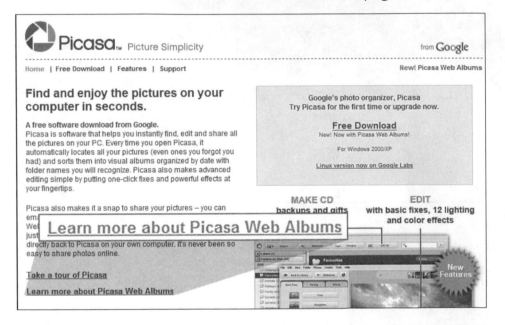

FIGURE 12.4
At the Picasa home page, you can learn more about the Picasa Web Albums.

All of the photo-sharing websites let you send the website address of your photos to others so they can see and enjoy your photos. It might require that they create a free user account on the site, but after they are registered, they can view any albums you choose to share.

Many of the photo-sharing websites offer other ways for users to inter-act with each other. As they offer more and more of these social net-working features, they are becoming more like online communities than just photo-printing websites. So be sure to check them out. You can use them to just post and share your photos, or you can become involved in some of the "community" aspects that appeal to you.

Fee-for-Use Sites

Websites such as ImageEvent charge a fee for their services because they have special additional capabilities, including large storage capacities, the ability to share videos, and the ability to use files of many different formats. ImageEvent charges $24.95 a year.

Smugmug is another account that charges a fee. At the time I write this, its fee is $39.95 a year. This site offers unlimited storage, special backups, and wonderful galleries with special slide shows and themes.

It may be worthwhile to pay a small amount to get extra services, but be sure to go with a service such as ImageEvent that has a free trial period. You will want to try out the service before you pay.

Travel-Focused Photo-Sharing Websites

Besides the usual photo-sharing websites, there are also special places for travelers to share their photos with other adventurers. The IgoUgo (www.igougo.com) Photo area has more than 200,000 travel photos. You can look through the wonderful photos of others to get ideas for photographic techniques, as well as to get a feel for a myriad of worldwide destinations. You can also upload your own photos and create your own albums.

Before you upload your photos to any website, be sure that you read the legal policies. For instance, you if you upload your photos to Discovery's Online Travel Channel at http://travel.discovery.com, you are agreeing that the pictures you send become the property of the site and can be used in a large variety of ways, as noted in the Legal Disclaimer at http://travel.discovery.com/yourshot/legal_1.html.

Online Travel Journals (Blogs)

Have you ever envied the travel writers who get to do nothing but travel around the world and write about it? Well, with the Internet and its many new resources, you can become a travel writer. You may not get paid for it, but you can have just as much fun, and you can share your travels with others with a new phenomenon called travel blogging.

LINGO

A *blog* is a personal journal that is posted on the Web. The word blog comes from we**b log**.

Blogging is just like creating an online journal, so it is perfect for keeping a travel journal. You can easily create a blog. Several websites allow you to publish a blog with just a few steps and no knowledge of Web languages or Web publishing. The Blogger website at www.blogger.com, shown in Figure 12.5, lets you set up your blog in less than 10 minutes, and everything is free. Here are the easiest and most popular websites where you can create a blog:

- Blogger: www.blogger.com
- LiveJournal: www.livejournal.com
- TypePad: www.typepad.com
- Vox: www.vox.com

All of these generic blogging tools let you create an online journal and let you post your entries whenever and from wherever you choose. They also allow you to easily post photographs in the blog, making them great tools for travel blogging.

Some travel blog sites provide additional tools that you may find valuable in creating a travel blog. The three most popular travel blogging websites are

- MyTripJournal: www.mytripjournal.com
- TravelPod: www.travelpod.com
- TravelPost: www.travelpost.com

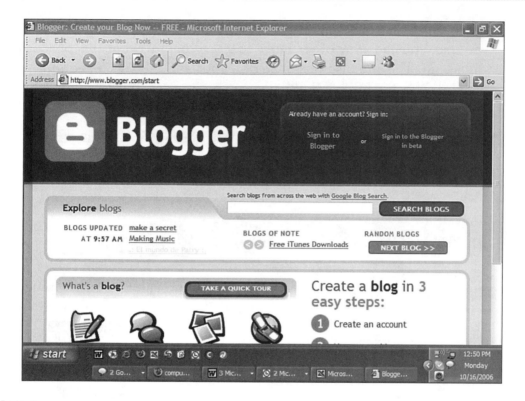

FIGURE 12.5
The Blogger website is a great place to start your blogging adventure.

As with the photo websites mentioned previously, some of these blogging websites are free and some have charges attached. The wonderful part about these blogging sites is that you can write your journal and upload your pictures while you travel using your laptop or some of the Internet cafés and hotel computers I talked about earlier in this book. This allows friends and family to trace your trip as it is happening and partake in the fun right along with you.

If you want to create a truly dynamic online travel journal, TravelPod is an excellent place to start. In addition to photos, you can also add audio and video files to your TravelPod blog. If you travel with a movie camera, this can create some spectacular results.

TravelPod has excellent information on how to create your blog, and, of course, you can view other blogs to get a feel for what this process is all about. The site also has a Guided Tour and a FAQs (Frequently Asked Questions) area that gives you even more helpful information. Figure 12.6 shows links to these areas.

FIGURE 12.6
The TravelPod website has a Guided Tour and a FAQs area to give you a quick overview of its services.

The little additional tools and services in TravelPod make it one of my favorites for travel blogging on the road. For instance, you can plot your travels on a map so that you can monitor your progress and so that friends and family can pinpoint your location. Also, TravelPod lets you keep a list of friends and family and automatically emails them when you update your travel blog.

The basic service at TravelPod is free, but you have to put up with some banner ads. If you make a one-time donation, your storage space increases. You get one additional megabyte of storage space for each dollar. You can eliminate the banner ads with a $20 payment, and $50 allows you to password-protect your blog so that it can be seen by only the people you authorize.

Again, you have to read the legal policies. As I write this, TravelPod retains the right to use your blog for promotional purposes. MyTripJournal, which charges a $59 yearly fee, lets you keep the rights to your posts and photos and allows you to password-protect your entire blog. The free TravelPost website lets you keep the rights to your posts and photos, but you can't password-protect your information.

As you can see, each website is different, and their rules can change at any time, so be sure that you read the legalese and familiarize yourself with their services before you post your information.

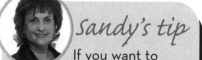

sandy's tip
If you want to post your pictures or email them home while you travel, purchase a USB card reader to transfer pictures from your camera to the computer so that you won't need special software or camera cables.

Sharing Your Memories When You Get Home

If you just want to take a vacation and not be bothered with documenting your progress or posting your email photos on the road, that's okay. Viewing and sharing your photos with others after you have returned from your vacation can actually help prolong the excitement of your trip.

With digital photography, you are not limited to viewing your photos after they have been returned from the photo-processing plant. Instead, you can use your computer to view, improve, and print your photos. If you took the perfect picture, but the subject has red eyes from the flash, you can quickly and easily remove it. I recently took a

picture at an awards ceremony that was too dark. Before digital photography, that photo would have gone in the trash. Instead, I opened it
on my computer and moved the light-adjustment slider on my photo-
editing software to lighten the picture until it was perfect.

Fixing Photos

A photo-editing program is software that enables you to make correc-
tions like the one I just described, as well as make complex changes
and improvements. For most consumers, a simple photo editor is all
you need. You may have received one with your computer or with your
digital camera. These programs often have the word "photo" or "picture" in the title. Some of the most popular are

- Photoshop Elements by Adobe: www.adobe.com

- PhotoImpact by Ulead: www.ulead.com

- Digital Image Suite by Microsoft: www.microsoft.com/products/
  imaging

- Photo Explosion Deluxe by Nova Development: www.
  novadevelopment.com

- Picasa by Google: http://picasa.google.com/

Most of these programs also have photo-organization capabilities that
allow you to caption and categorize your photos. This feature can come
in handy when you return home with a multitude of photos. You can
add keywords or tags to your photos so that you can easily look up a
group of photos just by searching for one word or phrase.

If you use a Mac, iPhoto comes with your operating system. It's full-featured image editing and organizing software. You can also purchase
bound albums and other print items from iPhoto.

If you don't have one of these programs, you can get one relatively easily. They range in price from about $29 to $99. You can also try a free
program called Picasa by Google, which I talked about earlier in this

chapter. You can download it at www.picasa.com. You will find it a full-featured photo-editing and photo-organizing program.

After you have tried some of these simple photo-editing programs, you can move on to more-advanced programs such as Adobe's Photoshop or Jasc's Paint Shop Pro. These more-expensive programs have a much longer learning curve, but they allow you to turn your photos into real works of art.

Printing Photos

As soon as your photos look the best they possibly can, you are ready to share them with others. There are many ways to do this. If you have a good ink-jet printer, you can print your pictures to share with others. If you don't have a capable printer, just upload your photos to Club Photo, Kodak Easy Share, Snapfish, Wal-mart.com, or any of the many photo-processing websites that print your photos and send them back to you by mail.

Many options are available for printing your photos. If you don't mind a trip to the store, you can take the media card out of your computer and take it to the photo kiosk at your local drugstore, superstore, or photo-printing shop, where they will print your photos for you.

> **LINGO**
>
> A *media* or *memory card* is a small removable storage card. It is often used to store images in digital cameras.

Creating Custom Photo Gifts and Scrapbooks

For lasting memories, all the online photo-printing websites and most local photofinishers can also print your photos on items such as coffee mugs, place mats, and T-shirts. Figure 12.7 shows just a few of the many photo gifts that are available at the Kodak EasyShare Gallery (www.kodakgallery.com). It can also create complete albums for you. If you are ambitious, you can create your own albums and photo scrapbooks. You can also purchase special paper for creating photos on fabric, magnets, and stickers. The list of what you can do with your digital photos is limited only by your imagination.

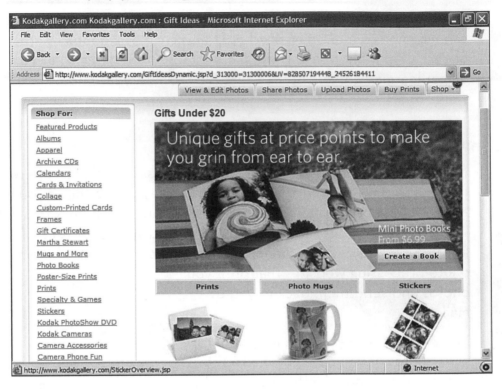

FIGURE 12.7
At the Kodak Gallery you can have your photos reproduced on mugs, stickers, and other paraphernalia.

Digital Scrapbooking or computer or electronic scrapbooking is a hot new way to create a scrapbook of travel memories. You can print your photos and use your computer to create a physical scrapbook by using different type styles, clip art, and paper. Or you can use your digital photos to create a completely digital scrapbook that appears on the computer screen. Both of these are popular and fun to do. There are many Internet resources that will help you.

You can start your digital scrapbooking with a simple word processing program like Microsoft Word, or you can us any of the photo editing programs that I mentioned earlier. There are also several dedicated scrapbooking programs like Ulead's My Scrapbook2 (www.ulead.com) or Hallmark's Scrapbook Studio Deluxe (www.hallmarksoftware.com) that can be very helpful in creating digital scrapbooks.

You can get more information on digital scrapbooking at the Digital Scrapbook Place at www.hallmarksoftware.com or The Scrapbook-Bytes at http://scrapbook-bytes.com.

Sharing Your Digital Video

Yes, we've come a long way since Super-8 videos and projection screens. Now you can take digital video with a digital video camera. Attach your video camera to your television with a simple cable and you can entertain your guests with your fantastic travel videos right on your television screen.

You can also enhance your videos on your computer. There are many software programs that will help you create wonderful documentaries of your travels complete with music and transitions. Two of my favorite are Adobe's Premiere Elements (www.adobe.com) and Ulead's VideoStudio (www.ulead.com).

Other High-Tech Ways to Share Your Travel Photos

There are many high-tech ways to show off your photos. Many of these are very easy to implement. For instance, I share my photos with others using my iPod. Although the iPod is known as a music player, many have screens that can display pictures.

When I return from an excursion, I transfer my photos to my iPod and carry it in my purse or briefcase to have my precious photos always available. When I don't have any travel photos, my iPod becomes Grandma's brag book, filled with my best family pictures.

Many iPods, cameras, and video cameras can be hooked up to your television so that you can invite friends over to see your travel pics without having to set up a screen or play around with projectors and slides.

There are even high-tech ways to share your photos with friends and family who don't have a computer. CEIVA Logic, Inc. (www.ceiva.com), shown in Figure 12.8, has a picture frame that you can purchase for friends and relatives who are not online. The CEIVA frame looks like a lighted picture frame and can display a slide show of photos. It hooks up to an ordinary telephone line, which is used to transfer the photos. You access the picture frame from your computer. Just upload your photos to the CEIVA website, and they automatically appear on your recipient's CEIVA picture frame. Although there is a monthly charge for this service, it's an easy way to share your photos over a long distance when you have a computer but the recipient doesn't.

FIGURE 12.8
The CEIVA picture frame lets you share photos with friends and family, even if they don't have a computer.

Another way to do this is with a system like that provided by Celery at www.mycelery.com. To use Celery, your recipient needs an inexpensive copier/fax machine that hooks up to her telephone line. With the Celery service, the person gets an email address, like greatgrandma@mycelery.com. Anyone can then send her a message or photograph by email. They can also send a handwritten note. When you use your email to send a picture or message to great-grandma's Celery account, she gets a telephone call from Celery, followed by the message, which appears in her fax/copy machine.

Several other companies are working on similar services, making it easy to share photos with those who do not have a computer and who don't like waiting for snail mail.

Sandy's Summary

Today there are newfangled ways to do everything. Sometimes that is very good, such as when you want to take digital photos of your trip and share them with others.

The Internet is a great resource for learning how to take good travel photos. With digital cameras you can easily get that perfect shot, and you don't have to wait for your photos to be developed.

You can share your photos by uploading them to the Web during your trip. You can even create a travel blog so that friends and family can learn about your trip as it happens.

When you get home, you don't have to set up the projector or deal with shoeboxes full of photos or slides. You can transfer your photos to your computer and create instant slide shows. Or you can hook up your camera to your television to create your own TV entertainment.

Today you can even share your photographic memories with distant friends and relatives through email, photo-sharing websites, and services that can electronically transfer your photos to even those who don't own a computer.

Sandy Berger

Index